MONARCH
PRESS

How to Be a Better Manager in 10 Easy Steps

George T. Doran, Ph.D.

MONARCH PRESS

NEW YORK

Published by MONARCH PRESS
A Division of Simon & Schuster, Inc.
Simon & Schuster Building
1230 Avenue of the Americas
New York, New York 10020

MONARCH PRESS and colophon are registered
trademarks of Simon & Schuster, Inc.
Designed by Irving Perkins Associates
Manufactured in the United States of America
10 9 8 7 6 5 4 3 2 1

Library of Congress Catalog Card Number: 83-61849
ISBN: 0-671-49388-4

Contents

Preface

It has been my good fortune to work with senior executives, managers, supervisors and business owners throughout our great country. I've been involved in various problem situations with people of different skills, temperaments and philosophies.

This pluralistic experience has convinced me that all organizations are unique in a personal sense. However, from the point of view of companies finding their direction and structure, employee problems, communication problems, and dealing with the transition from the family-owned, autocratic business to corporate organizations, these situations are not as unique as many managers assume. But given the real-world fact that managers and supervisors have different ideas, skills and expectations as to what their jobs really are, and given the fact that they operate in different markets with different technologies and different mixes of organizational structure and climate, all companies are unique. I've yet to come across the same situation mix in my 20 years of managing and consulting.

Nevertheless, what progressive organizations and individuals have in common is the need to increase their management effectiveness. It is *management* that makes the difference between success and failure. Operationally, this means that managers and supervisors have a need to develop their management-process skills, and skills in communicating, motivating their people, planning, organizing, staffing, directing and controlling.

Understanding this practical need is my ostensible motivation for writing this book. I want to capture and distill the diversified experience accumulated for pragmatic use in a wide variety of organizations. However, I also have another motivation. It's just something I want to do. I have learned techniques and practices from a great number of people. Now it's time for me to pay back and make my contribution to professional management. My hope is that this book will give managers, supervisors, business owners and others interested in management the practical tools and skills for success, direction and structure.

As author, I accept full responsibility for all ideas expressed in this book. As an organization-development consultant, I know that these ideas will increase your skills and professionalism. It doesn't matter what type of business you are currently engaged in or your management position. The ideas presented will be valuable to your career path and will result in a profitable return to your organization.

This book would not have been written if it weren't for the full support of my wife, Betty. She deserves my greatest appreciation and recognition. My two sons, Kevin and Sean, are also to be thanked for the time taken away from them during the writing of this book. I'd also like to thank my editor, Valerie Levy, for her commitment to this project. I've been most impressed with her professionalism. It has also been my good fortune to become associated with the Monarch Press division of the Simon & Schuster publishing company. This publishing company is an organization that demands and supports excellence. This book, therefore, is a combined effort of many professionals whose commitment is to serve you, the readers of this publication.

Introduction

How You Can Benefit From This Book

There are three types of people:
Those who make things happen,
Those who watch things happen and
Those who wonder what happened.
            —ANONYMOUS

This book is your survival and personal development guide. Because what you don't know can hurt you! It can hurt your career path, your operation, your company or organization. Much like lacking knowledge of radar and trying to fly a plane, the consequences could be disastrous. In a similar way, attempting to run a business or your own area of operation with Wright Brothers management can be equally disastrous. This book, therefore, is your radar to help you set a profitable, productive and successful business course. It will help you fly into a better future. It will help you make the important jump from doing to managing.

Your challenge today and in the future will be to seize opportunities, adopt and grow. This book will help you. It takes a hands-on approach for immediate use. It is not filled with academic theories, but with time-tested practices that will improve your effectiveness. It is written without the usual technical jargon and terminology. It is written in a clear and direct language that communicates. It is a valuable resource and reference edition for you. It has been purposely designed to be used and digested one chapter at a time. You have the flexibility to choose the chapter of your highest

3

priority or interest. If your need is for knowing how to set goals and objectives, you will discover that the chapter dealing with that subject *shows* you how to do it rather than just stating that setting goals or objectives is important. If your need is for determining your direction and structure, see the chapter on planning. If your need is for practical tips on how to motivate your employees, see the chapter on effective strategies for employee motivation.

The total manager understands that management means getting results. It means accomplishing your objectives. It means planning and taking risks. It means leaving an impact on society. It means anticipating and shaping the future rather than waiting for it. It means leadership. It means action. It means knowing how to select the best people for your organization. It means taking on the responsibility of obtaining results through coordinating the efforts of people. It means giving positive feedback to your people, and recognizing them for their accomplishments. It means control. It means knowing your customers. It means good communication. And it means your effective and efficient problem-solving and decision-making ability in the use of limited resources to achieve desired results.

The bottom-line objective of this book for the manager is your business or career success. It shows you how to maximize productivity, increase your effectiveness and company profits. It puts at your disposal the thinking that is needed for success.

The total manager knows that results are what employers want. Your career path will be insured if you can demonstrate your skills and ability to produce results in those areas of concern to your employer. Your boss is not interested in excuses, dreams or hopes. The boss is interested in what you produced since you came on board.

Can you manage change? Can you introduce change? Do you make your own opportunities? Are you preparing for your future? What is different now that you are on the scene?

WHAT MAKES YOU
AND YOUR ORGANIZATION TICK?

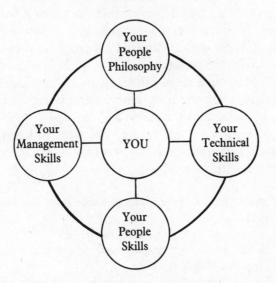

The fact that you are interested in this book tells me that you are a manager, a soon-to-be manager, a supervisor, a business owner, a business student or someone who is interested in professional management. You are interested in improving your skills, and you realize that businesses and other organizations operate in an uncertain and complex world. Consequently, you want to develop a management perspective that will guide you through turbulent weather, normal and good times. It doesn't matter where you are in the management triangle or what your current position is. Achieving results is the predicator of your success in any organization.

Most of what is written by academic types is written to impress other academic types. This book isn't written to impress, but to ensure that the message is received. Its essential ingredient is precise and concise communication. It is written to show you how to do those things that get results. It gives in nontechnical terms the practices of successful businessmen and women that when implemented will be bench marks in your career.

This book is also unique in that it utilizes a workbook strategy. It is not a book that tells you to see your Vice-President of Personnel (Human Resources) for people problems or to hire a consultant. It is a workbook designed to obtain your active involvement in problems that concern you. It gives you the nitty-gritty, step-by-step procedures that are practiced in profitable and successful businesses.

If you desire a better future, you want to know where you are, where you are going and how to get there. With this in mind, this book will:

- Show you how to introduce change into your business.
- Assess your management effectiveness.
- Develop your own management perspective.
- Organize your business.
- Distinguish between management work and operating work.
- Put more money in your pocket.
- Improve your communication ability.
- Teach you how to motivate people.
- Make you a results-oriented manager or supervisor.
- Control your costs.
- Improve your productivity, cash flow and profits.
- Manage your time more efficiently.
- Improve problem-solving and decision-making skills.
- Impress upon you the fact that, if you want a future, you must record the present.

Your future depends upon your awareness and understanding of how you manage yourself, your employees and your organization. This book is your road map to making your future brighter. Good luck!

ACTION STEP
1

How to Survive and Succeed in the Management Jungle

Success is a product of unremitting attention to purpose.
—Benjamin Disraeli

It all starts with a vision and a plan of action. A vision to identify opportunities, and a plan to invest a part of each day in reaching your personal and organizational goals. A vision of what must be done in your organization and an action plan to do it. Survival in the management jungle means that you must come down from your ivory tower, work smarter than most people, understand your environment, be flexible and anticipate and circumvent dangerous situations.

Successful business people think and act differently from nonsuccessful people. They think differently in how they manage their work, how they use key resources and how they take risk. Successful business people can look at an organization, a piece of property or a market and see what it can become.

Successful people are action oriented and interested in solving problems rather than placing blame. Successful people have a good understanding of their strengths and weaknesses. Much like Beowulf, the classic tale of good and evil, successful people draw strength *from* their weaknesses. In recognizing their limitations, they are able to maximize their strengths. Successful people recognize that the growth of

7

their business or organization is a reward for their achievements, and that all of their activities must be directed and coordinated with the overall objective of economic performance in mind.

The situation is basic. If you are to survive and grow as a manager or supervisor in the management jungle, you must keep one eye on what you are doing and one eye looking up at the needs of senior management. Many managers and supervisors fail because they don't think about understanding the total organization. They suffer from department myopia.

SUCCESS SYSTEM

Senior management must pass along or develop a management philosophy or strategy of how to succeed for their managers and supervisors.

Managers and supervisors must keep one eye looking up to spot the needs of senior management and understand their total organization.

Managers and supervisors must keep one eye looking down to manage their operation well for economic performance.

However, it has been my experience to recognize the fact that senior managers often contribute to the failures of their front-line managers and supervisors. They assume that once they promote people into the managerial ranks, somehow magically these people understand the needs and concerns of upper management. Senior management is guilty of assuming that because these individuals have years of experience with the company, they know the jobs of management and know how to function as a manager or supervisor. It's a major jump from operator to manager or supervisor. Senior management has developed over time a philosophy or strategy on how to manage. But given the many demands placed on senior management, they often have little or no time to pass along a strategy of managing to their new managers or supervisors. Recognizing this need of senior management, this book is a tool for this management group to distribute to their front-line managers and supervisors. It will develop a philosophy and strategy of managing no matter what organization is involved. Senior management must do all they can do to prepare their achievers with resources for their success. It should not be forgotten that their success is your success.

WHAT INVESTMENT IS NECESSARY FOR SUCCESS?

Just because you have been successful in the past, this doesn't guarantee the future will be more of the same. Your target markets are constantly changing, and consequently your success depends upon your ability to identify opportunities, motivate key people effectively and anticipate the challenges and trends affecting your area of operation. Effective and successful managers have learned that you manage things through systems, but that you lead people through your vision and action. If you take a militaristic approach to manage people, you will not succeed. If you push too hard, they will find creative ways to push back. Instead, take action on matters and problems of concern, and people will follow you.

Therefore, decide today that you will improve your performance and accomplishments by understanding what makes your organization tick, and what the success factors are in your particular situation. Decide today that you will set priorities and take actions to improve your decision-making and communication skills. Decide today on a plan of action for your personal and professional development. Success is achieved by breaking down your goals into smaller pieces. Take one step each day, and in ten days you will have taken ten steps to becoming a better and more successful manager.

No one individual is expected to have all the experience, knowledge and skills necessary for management excellence. However, high-achievement performers have individual and work characteristics that separate them from all others. To develop these success characteristics, you should work in the following ways:

1. Do More Than What Is Expected.

Spend at least 30 extra minutes each day accomplishing your work objectives. Anyone can put in the required number of hours at work. It's what you put into the hours that spells success. The successful person lives by the proverbial adage "I must be a little bit better." Work smarter than what most people are willing to do. Don't work on projects for which you lack training or ability. If you allocate your energies on those projects or activities that you cannot do well, you will neglect what you must do to manage or supervise a viable operation.

2. Develop a Simple Outline of Where You Want to Be at the End of the Year.

Managers and supervisors often neglect this action as a result of becoming too engaged in day-to-day operations. Consequently, six months from now they are no further ahead than today. Your tendency to neglect planning will result in ineffective and undirected action for your company. Get your people involved in this process. Successful people have found that their own employees can not only give direction, but can also supply recommendations and solutions to company problems. Don't fail to recognize and make use of the full capabilities of your employees. Without a plan, you and your employees can't make good decisions, since your direction and structure are not known. In addition, the planning process will enable you to recognize change, introduce change and adapt to it.

3. Periodically Audit Yourself.

Are you constantly putting off the difficult or unpleasant job that must be done? Are you flexible in your thinking in terms of new situations, ideas and people? An audit is a kind of checking up on your actions, behavior and progress. Managers and supervisors usually understand the need for financial audits in business in order to grow and, sometimes, survive. However, few realize the importance and need of a management audit for success. You may have great drive, skill and vision, but being human you also have weaknesses. Each week, review your accomplishments and write down what you want to accomplish for the next time period. Ask for feedback from your boss and peers so that you may better assess your strengths and weaknesses and take corrective action.

4. Set Goals/Objectives and Priorities.

Employees have a need to be part of an organization that knows where it has been and where it is going. Without a goal/objective-setting process your employees will be confused as to your expectations of them. Consequently, productivity will not be as high as it could be. With a goal/objective-setting process, managers, supervisors and operating personnel will better realize that working together and analyzing what they are going to do before they do it is a formula for success.

Don't keep your thoughts locked up inside your own mind and somehow expect that your people will know what you are thinking. Sometimes all it takes is putting up a bulletin board to inform your people of what's happening and what's planned.

Still better is to set aside a small amount of time, perhaps each Monday morning at nine o'clock, for a meeting with your key people. You can dry-run some of your ideas to see if they are workable and acceptable. This type of meeting is also a good coordinating mechanism. Your people will be informed of other departments' activities and how they can contribute to the goals and objectives of your organization. Your job then is to indicate your coming priorities and have your organization focused on accomplishment of those tasks necessary to a successful program.

5. Develop a Positive Mental Attitude, Have Enthusiasm and Be Proud of Your Work.

We are not born with attitudes, but we develop them as we journey through life. Successful people have learned not to worry about failure, but to believe in themselves and look for opportunities where other people see problems. They have a let's-get-going attitude, not a that-won't-work attitude. When you have this attitude, you create a work environment that in itself is stimulating. Negative-attitude people tend to attract other negative people, and the result is almost always failure. Your attitude is as important to your people as it is to your success.

In addition, if you want to be successful, be enthusiastic. Nothing great has ever been achieved without enthusiasm. Finally, when you are proud of your work, you will find ways to do it better and this way make a contribution to yourself, your organization and society.

6. Jointly Make a List of Results You Want to Achieve With Each Employee and Follow Up with Feedback.

If you are serious about making your operation or business more effective, profitable and responsive to change, a results philosophy is necessary. This means constantly looking for improvement, but not perfection, from your employees. Give your employees recognition for the results they have achieved. However, sit down and discuss with the person involved what parts of the project he or she feels could be done better the next time. This approach lets people know what you see of value in their work, and let's them participate in ways that their work can be improved. You and your employees must jointly determine what results can be reasonably expected within a specific time frame. The idea is to keep refining what is to be done. Conditions change, and consequently expected results should also change. Results-oriented people want to know whether or not they are on the right track.

7. Select the Best People and Motivate Them.

The productivity of your people will be one of the most critical factors in the success of your operation or business. Productivity begins with knowing how to select people. It surprises me, and maybe it may surprise you, that many managers and supervisors believe that they know how to select good people. However, when questioned about their approach, it becomes obvious that their system was in reality a hit-or-miss approach. In this book, we will look at a time-tested systems approach to the selection of personnel that will not only increase productivity but will also help avoid those problems you would have experienced by selecting the wrong people.

8. Set Standards of Performance and Avoid Your Comfort Zone.

The key to developing your employees is the level of expectation you set for them. If you set standards too low, your employees will become complacent and not be motivated to work hard. On the other hand, expectations set too high are self-defeating. Employees will realize that whatever efforts they make will never be enough. This will result in high turnover, lack of motivation and absenteeism.

Standards of performance should be as realistic and understandable as par on a golf course. Your job lies in communicating these clear expectations. Your employees should know as they come to the 18th green (or sooner) how well they are doing and where improvement is needed. Jointly developing a job description for this action step is a good place to start in setting work standards of performance.

Successful individuals are motivated by goals that they set for themselves. Less successful people find a comfortable home in meeting minimum standards. The successful performers are not satisfied in reaching a plateau, but constantly strive to improve their management and leadership skills.

9. Delegate Work, Responsibility, Authority and Accountability.

Delegating is often difficult for managers and supervisors because of the human tendency to believe that you can do it better than anyone else. This may be true, but you can't do all the work yourself. You must let others develop themselves and take care of the details. Learning to delegate is difficult, and some never learn how to do it. However, when you feel comfortable with delegating, you will learn that delegation will be a key factor in your success. Responsibility (work obligation) can be delegated, since you can make the subordinate obligated for the work tasks. In a similar way, authority (right to command) can be delegated, since you reserve the right to retract the delegation. The problem arises when you give your subordinates responsibilities but give them little or no authority. Finally, you can delegate accountability (answering for results) since your subordinates must answer to you. Although delegating may be difficult at first, you will find it one of your most rewarding management experiences. Become a master in the art of delegation.

10. Develop Your Problem-Solving and Decision-Making Skills and Take Moderate Risk.

Allocate between 15 to 30 minutes each day to studying some aspect of your job. With the knowledge gained, you will have the confidence needed for effective problem solving and decision making. Within a short period of time you will master your job and be ready to take on new challenges.

The business environment always has its risks and opportunities. Successful people have learned that they must take risks to succeed, but their risks must be moderate and calculated. When your hunches tell you that the downside risk is minimal and the upside potential is good, then move ahead with confidence. Those managers who don't analyze their maximum loss will probably not be successful.

11. Manage Your Time.

It's been said that if you don't manage your time, time will manage you. Make a things-to-do-today list in order of priority and stick to that list. Don't just react to whatever comes to your attention. In addition, knowing how you spend your time on work-related activities and with whom you spend your time is equally important. Don't be a victim of occupational myopia—spending most or all of your time with the same people.

Take time to read and study in areas that are not directly related to your business. These areas will always be a source of creative ideas for you. Don't get caught in the busy trap and postpone taking time out to smell the roses.

12. Improve Your Interpersonal Communication Skills.

When managers and supervisors really make efforts to communicate to their operating people, and when these people feel free to communicate back, energy is exchanged and the business becomes both economically and socially more productive.

In the movie *Cool Hand Luke*, Paul Newman uttered a classic line just before he was shot between the eyes in a churchyard: "What we got here is a failure to communicate." Definitely, this was a dramatic example of a failure to communicate. But you can never learn enough about communication. In fact, your success in life as well as on the job will largely depend upon your performance in this area.

13. Exercise a Little Each Day.

For a high level of energy, walk, jog, stretch, do isometric (without movement) or isotonic (actual movement) exercises. Try to maintain your body in good to excellent physical shape. It will pay dividends in your career path.

14. Have Cost Consciousness.

Managers and supervisors should recognize that controlling costs is a continual and ongoing responsibility. Cost consciousness is not the same concept as cost cutting or cost reduction. A cost consciousness is a realization that someone or some company is out there developing a product that is going to compete against your company's product and maybe put your product out of business. Consequently, you want to monitor all costs to keep yourself and your company viable. A cost consciousness is not falling into the trap of no limit on expense accounts when business is good. A cost consciousness means looking at every cost in relation to profit contribution. A cost consciousness is a long-run philosophy on cost. Cost cutting or cost reduction is short-run effort and usually the result of the cut costs by 10 percent mandate.

Managers and supervisors must keep a continuous emphasis on cost control, and not a once or twice push to control business costs. Effective managers and supervisors exercise a cost consciousness not by their monthly lecture but by their behavior commitment and example in controlling costs.

As a manager or supervisor, you must realize that *you* are your own key to success. It's so easy to point the finger at someone else, economic conditions, declining markets or other factors. But if you are to be successful, it will take smarter work, creativity and imagination. It will also take self-criticism and an attitude of never quitting or being satisfied with your present performance. You must be proud of your work and honest about your strengths and weaknesses.

ACTION EXERCISE

Given the fourteen suggestions on how to survive and succeed in the management jungle, choose two areas that you feel you are weak in and write out your preliminary thoughts for taking action in these two areas.

ACTION STEP

2

How to Establish a Management Strategy for Yourself

Business is like war in one respect; if its grand strategy is correct, any number of tactical errors can be made and yet the enterprise proves successful.

—GENERAL ROBERT E. WOOD
  (when president of Sears)

Professional athletes know that when they do the ordinary in an extraordinary way, they will be winners. They have developed routines or a series of steps that become their strategy in making them and their team winners. For managers and supervisors desiring to establish a personal strategy, it is important to realize that strategy is a lot like knowing how to be a winner. It answers the questions: How do I win? What methods must I use to achieve my objectives? What will move my organization toward the attainment of our goals?

Professional basketball players will shoot thousands of shots to find out where they are most effective. Professional golfers will spend hours perfecting their short game. When Tom Watson chipped in his golf ball from out of the rough on the 17th and last hole of the U.S. Open, he knew what he had to do to win. He was aware of his options, and he picked the right one. A professional baseball player will spend countless hours going over and over the fundamentals of the game. A professional tennis player will hit bucket after bucket of balls attempting to improve his or her ground stroke and serve. A professional bowler knows how to adjust the line, speed and proper roll as lane conditions change during a tournament. What do all of these professionals have in common? They have a strategic process that makes them winners. They know what they have to do as their environment or conditions change. They also recognize that there is no single best way to do what they have to do.

Likewise, as a manager or a supervisor or as a business owner, it should be recognized that there is no one best way to manage your people and your organization. Your management strategy should be viewed as a game plan that provides you with a tool to be a winner. In the real world, there are no instant replays. You want your future to be better. You can't rely on theories, you have to do it right the first time.

Those managers and supervisors who operate without a management process will not effectively manage their jobs, and consequently their jobs will manage them. Without a process, you will spend your time fighting fires and not managing your business or operation. You will be confused as to what is management work and what is operating work. You won't have time to develop policies and effective plans and think about structuring work that will give you more time. You won't have time to do things right, because you will be making the same mistakes over and over again. It is therefore important to realize that the development of a strategy for yourself is a disciplined process that involves getting results through other people. Profit from the experience of professional managers who have developed a sequence of actions that makes them winners. Realize that you will not live long enough to learn everything through your own experience. If you don't develop a strategy to guide you in your decision making, you will be like a ship without a rudder. Consequently, before you realize it, your career path and the profitability of your organization will fall upon the rocks of hard times.

From the general who organized the Persian invasion of 490 B.C. to modern-day professional managers and supervisors success or failure depends upon understanding yourself and those around you. To get started in the development of a management strategy for yourself take Aristotle's advice: Know Thyself.

YOUR MANAGEMENT-STRATEGY PROCESS

1. Know Thyself and Thy Environment.

A sage once said that you can only really know yourself by what other people tell you. Successful achievers want to know how they are doing. They want to know how they are doing with their peers and with their boss. Operationally, they ask the question: How am I doing? The answer to this question gives managers and supervisors a perspective on their strengths, weaknesses, opportunities and problems or threats in their organization. The importance of knowing yourself cannot be overstated. As human beings, we probably will never get to know ourselves completely, but as professionals we must learn to play within our limitations and strengths. Your understanding of your strengths and limitations will be the glue that will hold your organization together. Without a proper understanding of yourself and your people, assumptions will be made to the detriment of your survival and growth. You must realize that your success and the success of your employees are related like the sides of a coin. One cannot succeed at the expense of the other.

It is also important to know the climate in your organizational environment. You may see yourself as a professional who wants to move the company into the 20th century. However, paranoia may develop among executives who see you as a threat to their comfortable way of doing things. If this should happen, you probably are not in the right organization.

2. Set Goals/Objectives and Priorities.

This action is usually a difficult one for managers, supervisors and business owners. The setting of objectives often represents a threat to the established way of doing things. Consequently, if you are like many managers or supervisors, you will think that you are too busy to set goals or objectives. For our purposes, think of goals as general statements of intention, e.g., to conduct your business with integrity. Objectives are specific and time-related results that you want to achieve. However, don't get caught in the semantic jungle. The important consideration is that you and your people decide upon a meaning of these terms within your organization.

Without setting objectives, you probably will be activity oriented, not results oriented. Consequently, you will develop an organization that generates a lot of activity but with few results. To help get yourself out of this dilemma, just think of the acronym SMART to help you write meaningful objectives. Objectives should be:

S	Specific.	Target a specific area for improvement.
M	Measurable.	Quantify or at least suggest an indicator of progress.
A	Assignable.	Specify who will do it.
R	Realistic.	State what results can realistically be achieved; give available resources.
T	Timely.	Specify when the result(s) can be achieved.

It should be pointed out that not all objectives can be quantified with precision on all levels of management. In certain situations, it is not realistic to attempt quantification, particularly in staff middle-management positions. Practicing managers and corporations can lose the benefit of a more abstract objective in order to gain quantification. Once your objectives have been determined, set priorities for these objectives.

3. Determine Action Steps and Procedures to Accomplish Your Objectives.

Once you set your goals and objectives, ideally with the participation for your key employees, it's time to take action. In the previous step, you have determined *what* results must be achieved by management if your organization is to function effectively and efficiently. Not it's time to determine which activities are necessary to reach your stated objectives. You want to know *how* to be effective and efficient. This is at the very heart of your strategy/process development. Because now you must make decisions on *how you are to get there*. Therefore, at this state you begin to translate activities into specific procedures. These procedures usually involve a detailed work plan that specifies the available human and financial resources, and the allocation of work by individual or organization unit. The setting of schedules for both your action program and its respective component parts are other decisions you must make in reaching your objectives. In all cases, your strategy involves a choice. That is, a choice of what particular actions, activities and procedures you will decide upon in determining the nature of your business and organization.

4. Structure Your Organization.

Do you fit the person to the job, or do you fit the job to the person? Do you create an organization that encourages people to accept positions where they will be productive, even if it means a lower position? Do you administer salaries to the job title or to the contributions that employees make? Do you hold your people accountable for their behavior. Does your organization structure promote teamwork and cooperation? Do you periodically make evaluations of job responsibilities—perhaps every other year? We live in an environment of rapid change, and consequently any organization that isn't thinking about changing its structure is probably a dying organization.

Your organization is the foundation of your effectiveness. Once you have determined how you will accomplish your plans, you must now build an organization structure. As manager/supervisor or business owner you will be more effective if you select people who fit the strategy (action plan) of your organization or company, rather than allow the current availability of people to determine the structure.

In structuring your organization, you want to establish a climate that improves the commitment of your people to their jobs. To accomplish this result, there are a few major considerations. First, you should analyze and compare all of the basic work processes involved in getting out the work. Scrutinize the contribution that each work process makes toward the attainment of economic goals. Second, review the current organization design for its strengths and weaknesses. Then derive alternative organization structures with their respective pros and cons. Reach a consensus as to the best alternative, and then implement the new structure. Finally, determine the facilities required to service your new organization structure, then develop a plan for managerial development of the people involved. It's important that your development program educate all those affected by the new arrangements.

Overall, you are trying to create an environment in which the organization becomes more effective and people have personal freedom to develop themselves. Implementing a management-by-commitment (MBC) system is the most highly effective means that I know of for you to accomplish this twin objective.

5. Establish Controls.

Probably the two best words that describe the word "control" are "no surprises." Put another way, control is the process of making sure that you and your organization attain your respective objectives. Control sets up the framework within which your people operate. When you are in command of this framework, you are in control. As you already know, people don't like to be controlled. So what is a manager or supervisor to do? Engineer a system into existence whereby people control themselves. Establishing a participative management process, whereby people have some say-so over decisions that affect them, leads to this type of control. Your effectiveness as a manager or supervisor will be greatly increased.

Effective managers in both the private and public sectors must anticipate problems and take corrective action *before* the problem or failure occurs. Although the word "control" often is associated with a negative meaning, a better understanding of control is to think of it as a positive concept. Control is forward looking. It will give you timely warning of potential fires. So instead of wasting your time and spending scarce resources on fire-fighting activities, you are managing your company and making profits.

Control from a manager's point of view can be best thought of as a system. A system with a few elements to help you achieve your objectives. It doesn't have to be complicated. Your control system can consist of just a few charts and some objectives. A few charts to measure output, costs or profit levels. Even in a profitable organization, if you don't control these factors you may be missing opportunities or you will lose your market position.

To develop your continuous control system, first establish some minimum level of expectation regarding the most important factors that must be controlled. You don't want to control everything. These minimum expectations are your work standards. Next you will need a method of comparing actual results to the established standards. As mentioned before, perhaps a simple chart is all that you need. I've found it productive to have such charts visible to those individuals whose work performance is being recorded. Finally, you need a means of taking corrective action. Corrective action may be nothing more than being a good listener. Find out the causes of the deviation, and then take corrective action. From an operating viewpoint, corrective action may mean the development or improvement of a management-information system. From a management viewpoint, standards may have to be changed to reflect the current environment. This will give you an opportunity to discuss with your people improved controls, methods and procedures.

In your control-process design, don't neglect thinking about the "human dimension." Use your control system to influence positive behavior. By jointly setting meaningful and realistic standards, you will initiate a desire among your people to develop and control themselves. Too much control, on the other hand, will have its negative effects. Birds and people want to be free to fly. If you attempt to control your people too closely, it will backfire. In fact, I've found it better to err on the side of less control than on the side of too much control. In summary, realize that the focus of your control system is to reach desired organizational objectives. Only in this way will you be in control. And make sure that your controls are appropriate to the situation at hand.

6. Execute Your Program and Motivate Your People.

Sometimes it isn't what you do but the way you do it that counts. If you like to do things for your people, you probably are not managing or developing your people. Your strategy should now involve getting things done through people. You want your people to do the things you want because they want to do it. This means that you must become a master of delegation. Even though you can do things better than your subordinates, you can't do it all. Many managers and supervisors find delegating as difficult as going to a dentist. However, if you are to be successful, you must learn the art of delegation. Don't tell your people how to work, just tell them the results you want and provide them with the necessary authority to accomplish the necessary work.

In addition to getting things done through people, your job also requires the motivation of your people. You must set a climate that is in itself motivating. By measuring the reaction of your people to policies and objectives, you will develop motivational skills. You will find out what "moves" your people and what doesn't. Develop a habit to constantly interpret and communicate changes in company goals and policies. Your employees will be motivated by your concern to keep them informed. Discover the motivation profile of each of your employees, and you will take a giant step in becoming a better and more effective manager/supervisor or business owner.

7. Follow-up, Feedback and Appraisal.

As with knowing yourself, the importance of follow-up, feedback and appraisal cannot be overstated. Your job is to plan your and your organization's future. This requires that periodic follow-up on plans and activities be scheduled. If you have a new employee in your group, more frequent follow-up will be necessary. If you are introducing change into your organization, more frequent follow-up will also be necessary.

Once you have followed up, praise your employees and give them the recognition that they deserve. You will find

YOUR STRATEGY AS
A TOTAL MANAGER

<u>A</u>

Know Thyself and
Thy Environment

<u>G</u>

Follow-up, Feedback
and Appraisal

<u>B</u>

Set Goals/Objectives
and Priorites

<u>C</u>

Determine Action Steps
and Procedures

<u>F</u>

Execute Program
and
Motivate People

<u>E</u>

Establish Control

<u>D</u>

Structure Your Organization

your effectiveness increasing as you give more credit for things that go right and take the blame when things go wrong. Following up will help you ensure that you are meeting your organization's needs, and positive feedback will help keep your employees motivated.

Finally, in the appraisal process you are attempting to evaluate how effectively you are using your organization's limited resources, i.e., human and financial resources, in meeting your objectives. Follow the formula of always trying to maximize the strengths of your people and minimize their weaknesses. You can do very little about other people's weaknesses. And follow the return-on-investment (ROI) profitability criteria in appraising how you managed your financial performance.

Like the professional athlete, you now have a 7-step routine or strategy (action steps) to make you a winner. Establishing a management strategy for yourself will make you a better and more effective manager or supervisor.

ACTION EXERCISE

1. List your strengths.

2. List your limitations.

3. What are your most promising organization/business opportunities?

4. How will you capture and maintain these opportunities?

ACTION STEP

3

How to Plan and Set Objectives for Your Organization

The purpose of the work on making the future is not to decide what should be done tomorrow, but what should be done today to have a tomorrow.

—PETER F. DRUCKER

High-performance management demands planning. In fact, the creation of an effective plan will affect your performance and profitability more than any other single factor. Your most superb strategy can be no better than the thinking or planning that preceded it. Without planning you will become a captive of your own assumptions. Without planning you will experience a scotoma in your thinking. Without planning your organizational structure and people will not be able to respond quickly to change.

If you are like most managers and supervisors that I come in contact with, you are much better at directing and controlling functions. When it comes down to a choice between doing something else or sitting down and thinking about alternatives, improving the quality of information flow, gaining cooperation with others, we tend to neglect this most fundamental management function. Planning requires that you sit down and think about the forces and trends that are affecting your operation, your department or your company. For many of us, planning is outside our comfort zone, and, therefore, I suspect 90 percent of all managers would prefer to do activity work rather than planning. Consequently, it is no surprise that most businesses feel comfortable drifting rather than planning ahead for profit-making opportunities. A plan will help you avoid costly surprises and will give you and your people a systematic approach to developing your direction, structure and a profitable course.

WHY PLAN?

1. So you will be in control rather than controlled.

A company that I have become very familiar with came to the market with the right product at the right time. Growth and profits just took off. Although this should have been a time of joy, the business went out of control and almost went bankrupt. Unfortunately, this is a very common situation. Not knowing how to manage growth can put you out of business quickly. In this company, people who usually worked well together suddenly found themselves in serious conflicts with one another. Others who functioned as good Indians found it difficult to accept new responsibilities. Departments were exhibiting much energy but were all going in different directions. In addition, the general manager found it difficult to communicate his personal management philosophy and was losing touch with his people as the paperwork started building up. It wasn't till this general manager finally realized that his organization needed a formal planning system that the company was able to stop the decline and start putting some direction and structure back into the company.

2. So you can get results.

The basic job of a manager or supervisor is to get results. But how can your employees help you with the burden of getting results? How can your people come up with solutions and recommendations to minimize business risk and solve departmental or organizational problems? How can you co-ordinate the various sections under your control or depart-ments in your company so that they are all heading in the same direction? The problem is basic. The solution is a planning system. It is well known to successful companies, but it is one of the newest management tools for the small and growing businesses of our economy.

3. So you can recognize, introduce and adapt to a changing, complex world.

Change is a relevant issue for all managers and super-visors. For your organization to grow and survive you must periodically evaluate changes in your internal and external environment. A formal planning process is a good discipline to help you see the need for change and show you how to change your objectives in line with your changing environ-ment. Research has shown that high-performance individ-uals and companies use a formal planning process in their business. People and organizations are naturally reluctant to change, but when they participate in those changes af-fecting them they will be more accepting of the changes implemented in your operation or business.

4. So you can develop and recognize your people.

A football coach I know can have his team leading 24 – 0 in the second half and still be very reluctant to put in his reserves. To me this is not only poor football practice, it's also poor management. Someday you are going to have to rely on those other players. In the planning process, you can bring in new team players and observe what they can do. The experience enhances their managerial development and will pay dividends for you later on. People want to be part of an organization that knows where it is going. In team planning, the communication process is strengthened and people are being developed for future management responsibilities.

5. So you can make better operating decisions today.

If you know what you are aiming at, you have a much better chance of hitting the target. It's only when you don't know what to aim at that you get yourself into trouble. If your employees have a choice of doing Work A or Work B with a plan, they will know what decisions to make. Without a plan they have to guess and may make the wrong decision. There are other benefits to the planning process, but if you keep these five benefits in mind, the time it takes to plan will well be worth its cost.

HOW TO GET STARTED IN THE PLANNING BUSINESS

It takes imagination and creativity if your operation is going to respond to change and survive. Consequently you want a flexible system that is workable, realistic and simple to understand. Therefore, a key ingredient in this planning system is a realization that it must fit your needs. You and your team must be the model builders. In your system, your first decision must be to decide *who* will do the planning. This implies a team approach to planning. The concept that the boss should do the planning and the employees the implementing is dangerous. If you think of your employees as only a pair of hands and not as also having a mind, you are getting started on the wrong foot. Therefore, if you want to realize the best return on your wage and salary investment, the team approach is the only reliable and consistent way to go. With this philosophy, you will improve employee productivity overall and discover that you have established a climate that leads to the motivation and commitment of your people to their jobs.

In the management planning language, the first phase of a planning process answers the question: Where are you? To answer this question you first come up with a vision/ mission statement and establish a procedure for analyzing the internal and external forces affecting your organization. You then establish your purpose and analyze your strengths, limitations and opportunities. In short, you want to know your corporate fitness.

The following steps should be taken to achieve effective planning:

Step 1   Development of a Vision/Mission Statement

One of the most important tasks of top management is to identify the specific purpose of the organization. Without an acceptance of this basic purpose by key people, there can be no effective planning. However, the activity of thinking through the reason for the existence of your operation is so basic that many managers skip over this planning step. It is ignored because the assumption is made that your people must know what the purpose of their department or organization is. Unfortunately, when managers or supervisors are questioned about the basic purpose of their departments, you often receive as many different opinions as there are managers and supervisors.

The word "vision" implies the power of seeing. It also suggests imagination or a mental picture that gives you an insight. For example, are you in the cosmetics business, or are you in the beauty business? Are you in the toy business, or are you in the youth-entertainment business? Unless your team can agree upon and see in their mind's eye what the basic purpose of their department or organization is, your profit planning will just be an exercise. The determination of your purpose will guide your organization into the setting of goals—effective objectives—and implementing the proper strategy to achieve results. The task of coming up with a vision/mission statement will have strategic consequences for your organization. It will be the invisible hand that helps determine your direction and structure. ·

Step 2 Development of Goals

A goal is a general statement of expectation about the direction in which a manager, business owner or executive wants to take the company. In this sense, a goal rarely has a time frame, usually isn't measurable and may never actually be achieved. A goal such as providing courteous, prompt and reliable service to our customers is an example of the above criteria. Such a goal is as important to a small retail/wholesaler as it is to a medium-sized computer keyboard manufacturer or a large Fortune 500 company. Most people only perform as well as they are expected to. The setting of expectations through goals will improve employee productivity and overall performance.

Examples of goals include: (1) conducting all business activities with honesty, fairness and integrity; (2) establishing an environment that encourages, assists and rewards employee development and achievement; and (3) taking a leadership role in community activities and practicing good business citizenship. Goals, therefore, reflect your values, beliefs and philosophies. Your establishment of goals will be the umbrella that protects and guides your organization.

Step 3 Subordinate Input and Environment Analysis

Good planning is based on factual information concerning all of those forces and factors affecting your key managers and supervisors. Unfortunately, information doesn't exist in such obvious form that you can easily identify your problems and opportunities. Identifying problems and opportunities is not as easy as picking an apple from a tree. No problem can be solved until its existence is comprehended, and no opportunity can be gained if you don't have an action plan to achieve it. Your operation's problems and opportunities can only be found in the expertise and thoughts of your people. You must learn to tap this gold mine of creativity and innovation if you want to survive profitably. You must in a systematic manner draw out the expertise and thoughts of your people who are closer to your customers and financial statements. In asking for your subordinates' input you will discover that your employees' ideas and

SUBORDINATE INPUT

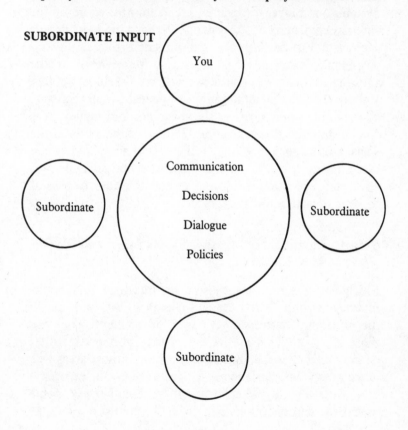

thoughts will be most helpful in developing solutions to your organization's problems.

A good environment analysis involves looking at both the external and the internal factors and forces that have a direct effect upon the success and health of your operation. The external environment comprises such factors as technology, government regulations, raw-material problems, changing customers and market conditions, the economy, etc.— many factors over which you have no control. The internal environment is really the interrelationships of your operations and company. Factors such as the management process, organization structure, budgetary process, information systems, employee programs, etc. comprise some of the internal environment subsystems. Perhaps the most important system in the internal environment is the administrative-management process. It is also referred to as the information–decision–influence system. You must not lose sight of the fact that although your operation is an aggregate of men and women, materials, machines and money, it is first of all a social organization. Therefore, be aware of the social factors such as power, jealousy and acceptance when designing systems. Without an environmental scanning process, your operation will lose messages that may be critical to your present and future successes.

Step 4   Identification of High-Payoff Areas and SWOP Analysis

High-payoff areas are those areas in which you should invest your time, resources and energy so that you realize the maximum return on your work investment. They are those areas in which 20 percent of the effort produces 80 percent of the results. The identification of those areas will make a significant economic difference for your organization. By evaluating where you and your employees spend their time and energy you will achieve control over orga-

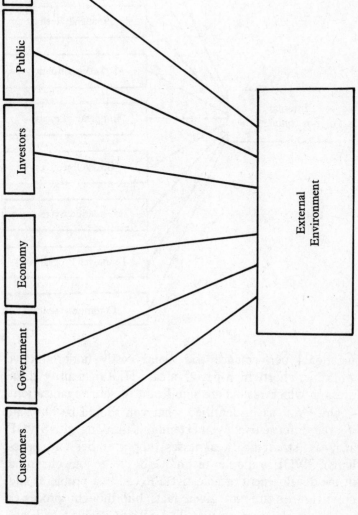

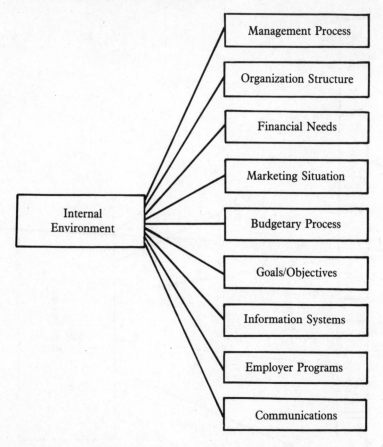

nizational performance and avoid costly nonproductive work. In short, high-payoff areas (HPAs) identify those areas in which results are significant to your organization.

Once you have identified what you should be busy at, it's very informative if you extend this thinking with SWOP analysis (strengths, weaknesses, opportunities and problems). SWOP is another technique or tool to jog your mind in the development of objectives. Recall that problems and opportunities are not given facts but thought processes locked inside your people. The SWOP analysis will add

WHAT ARE YOUR HIGH-PAYOFF AREAS?

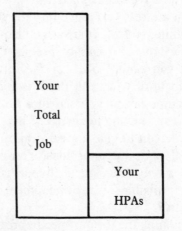

another dimension in figuring out the direction and structure of your organization. Therefore, you should consider a SWOP analysis for each HPA. This means that if you have five high-payoff areas, you should have five SWOP analyses. It is recommended that on the first go around seven HPAs should be your upper limit for this type of analysis.

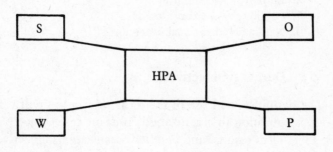

Step 5 Developing Planning Assumptions

Now that you have determined where your company is at present, you are ready to move into the second phase of the profit-planning system. It answers the question: Where do you want to go? You cannot predict the future with accuracy, but you cannot plan for the future unless you create an estimate of what you think is going to happen. You must attempt to put yourself in a position of anticipating rather than reacting to change. This situation makes it imperative for you to give a great deal of thought to the development of critical assumptions. You can think of an assumption as a temporary guess (hypothesis) regarding a very important probable future development over which you have little control.

Assumptions applying to your specific area could include:

1. Manpower requirements
2. Capital requirements
3. Market conditions
4. Social trends and forces
5. Government regulation
6. Raw-material supply sources
7. Technology
8. Employee communications
9. Public relations considerations
10. National and regional economics

Step 6 Deriving Objectives

The definition and use of the term "objective" will vary from organization to organization. In some cases objectives are short-term results, and in other organizations objectives are long-term results. An objective is a result expected to be achieved within some time frame. An objective is also a milepost directed toward the achievement of some goal. The exact label is not all that important. What is important is that your team agree on the terminology of what an objective is in your organization.

It should also be noted that objectives are based on assumptions. Once the planning assumptions have been formulated by the planning teams, their job is the development of company objectives. This is the second step in determining where you want to go.

Objectives are the very heart of your planning process. They provide guidance to managers and supervisors in making decisions in line with the aims and strategies of business owners and upper management. Without objectives, how can your managers make effective decisions?

Your objectives should meet criteria that you and your team deem important. However, as a guide to your thinking at this point in time, you should consider the following criteria: (1) you should specify a time frame in which objectives are to be accomplished; (2) you should specify end results; (3) objectives should be measurable so you know whether or not they have been achieved; (4) the individuals responsible should develop objectives that are attainable; and (5) you should have the resources necessary for realistic attainment. In addition, your objectives should be listed in order of priority.

Step 7   Action Plans

The development of action plans begins the third phase of the planning process. It answers the question: How are we to get there? In this author's view, the words "action plans" and "strategy" are synonymous. Strategies are the things we do and the methods we use to achieve our objectives. They also move us toward our goals. Our strategy and action plans become the instrument that transforms a theoretical plan into a dynamic and successful course of action.

The action plan worksheet enables you to specify the key

action steps to be taken in reaching your objectives. In specifying the steps on the right-hand side of the page, be sure also to indicate when each action step is to be completed. These action steps are your strategy for accomplishing results.

Action Plan Worksheet	
Objectives	Action Plan
1.	1 a.
	1 b.
	1 c.
2.	2 a.
	2 b.
	2 c.

Step 8   Management Review and Feedback

Feedback is the connecting link between a management review and planning future results. By reviewing what has happened and analyzing the reasons for such happenings, managers, supervisors, business owners and executives can use the experience gained to take the proper corrective action. In the review process we are looking back to see what has taken place, and in the feedback process we are communicating future moves to minimize mistakes or deviations and help ensure profitable planned results. Periodic management review is a necessary step in this system.

Step 9   The Planning Document

The final step in the planning process is the documentation of your team's planning efforts. This manual will serve you and your key people as (1) a reference manual,

(2) a guide to future planning and (3) an identification of development needs of the organization.

The amount of information contained and scope of contents will of course be determined by you and your key people. However, as a guide, here are some categories of information:

1. Overview of your planning process
2. Summary statement
3. Planning schedule
4. Mission statement
5. Goals
6. External/internal environment
7. Capabilities and business opportunities
8. Key assumptions
9. Objectives
10. Policies and procedures
11. Organization chart
12. Strategies
13. Budgets

It is not necessary to have all of these categories in your planning manual. Some categories can be combined or eliminated. Keep your planning simple. Use only those parts that benefit you.

ACTION EXERCISE

1. What is your plan?

2. What are the four or five key assumptions concerning your operation or business?

3. Who knows about them?

4. What are they going to do about it?

5. How will you know if your plan is working?

ACTION STEP
4

How to Motivate Your People

*If you treat a man as he is, he will
remain as he is. If you treat him
as if he were what he could be and
shall be, he will become what he
could be and should be.*

—GOETHE

You manage things, but you motivate and lead people. Napoleon may have had this in mind when he stated that "an army's effectiveness depended upon its experience, size, training and motivation...and that motivation was worth more than all the other factors combined." The real key to productivity improvement and profit performance lies in your ability to set a motivating climate for your people. This is true for all organizations. No matter how able your people, when motivation declines, so does performance.

Everyone has a reservoir of untapped energy. If you are to obtain results from your people, you must know how to turn on the motivational forces within your people and create an environment that encourages self-motivation. Motivation is not something you can pour into a person. Motivation requires an understanding of the changing needs and wants of people, leadership ability and an understanding of what makes a particular job rewarding to a particular individual.

Employees today want their managers or supervisors to listen to their opinions, give them credit for what they do and take an interest in their well-being. They want to do a good job, and they will do a good job when you let them know what is expected, appreciate their efforts, train them to perform, take time to know them as individuals and give them frequent and meaningful feedback as to how they are doing. Employees have many needs, and money is not the only motivating force. You can pay poorly and still have highly motivated people. On the other hand, you can pay well and still have no guarantee that your people will be motivated. Contemporary employees want to work in an organization that knows where it is going. They want to participate in decisions that are going to affect them. These employees want to work for a manager or supervisor who gives them the feeling that their opinion counts in the organization. Modern employees want their accomplishments recognized, want more control over events affecting their lives and want interesting work.

It has been my experience as a consultant, executive and manager over the past 20 years that the most highly motivated work forces are those in which the managers and supervisors develop a trust relationship with their people, lead by example, set joint performance standards and provide performance feedback in a positive manner. Employees want their managers or supervisors to meet their self-esteem needs, engineer meaningful work and exercise a certain amount of discretion or control over their operations. In short, employees want managers or supervisors with a positive attitude who treat people the way they want to be treated—with respect and appreciation.

MOTIVATIONAL STRATEGIES

1. Motivate Through Values.

Most people in their late 30s and older are meritocratic in nature. That is, they believe that hard work, loyalty, sacrifice and commitment today will result in a better tomorrow. Most individuals under 25 are equalitarian in nature and are often characterized as the I-want-it-now generation. The age group in between is mixed and has characteristics of both value systems. Younger employees have goals with a short-run time orientation, in contrast to the meritocratics, whose goal orientation is long-run. In addition, the equalitarians have been raised in a television/communication age with instant answers. Consequently, it's no surprise that they want better and faster communication from management as to what's happening within the organization. They also want work that is not boring but worthwhile and interesting. This instant gratification of the "younger generation" strikes a sour chord with "older generation" folks.

If you are of the meritocratic type, your strategy should be to talk regularly to your people about their jobs. Learn what they find interesting and challenging. Then, when it comes time to assign work, you will better realize that the job itself can be motivational to your selected employees. It's therefore important for you to be aware of your values and of your subordinates' values. By clearly setting joint short-run objectives and keeping communication lines open, you will be taking an important step in motivating your people.

2. Motivate Through Leadership.

General Eisenhower often demonstrated the art of leadership via a simple piece of string. He would place it on a table and then ask members of his staff to first push it and then pull it. He would then ask them what they had observed. It took more energy to push, and the string didn't seem to go anywhere. Pulling the string took a minimum of energy and it followed you wherever you went. The general explained that it's the same way when it comes to motivating people. Your job as a manager or leader is to create a climate in which your subordinates want to follow you because you know where you are going and because you have a plan and objectives. You are then able to communicate to employees how they can meet their own objectives while at the same time meeting organizational objectives. Effective leaders know that they can best motivate their people by working through them and helping them achieve more than they thought possible.

Realize that for every action there is a reaction. If you constantly push your people into doing work, they will find ways to push back. They can creatively avoid work, slow down or misinterpret your instructions.

Your leadership strategy is to develop a work-objective contract with your employees. This work contract allows employees to get results through their own initiative. The job of leadership is not to tell your people exactly what to do and how to do it. Instead, the job of leadership is to create a work climate that in itself is stimulating. If you find that you are spending a good portion of your time pushing, you are not leading.

3. Motivate Through Group Influence.

The day-to-day interactions of workers with their fellow employees has a very important impact on employee motivation and productivity. The famous Hawthorne Experiment, conducted at a Western Electric plant in the 1930's, brought this social fact to light. The psychologists conducting the experiment intended to measure the importance of the physical environment on workers, but found that an employee places important weight on his or her peer status, i.e., how he or she appears to his or her fellow workers. Work groups give status, a sense of belonging and praise. Work groups also satisfy ego needs. It is therefore important for managers and supervisors to be aware of these informal groups so that they can be managed and directed properly.

These informal work groups can be an important motivation tool. In the past, emphasis had been placed on the formal group (formed by management and visually presented by the organization structure) as the way to increase productivity and motivation. It should now be obvious that this approach has only been marginally successful in present circumstances.

Your strategy is to promote a healthy motivational attitude by encouraging the formation of informal work groups. Identify the natural leaders of these groups and establish a trust relationship between the leader and yourself. You then can communicate work expectations through this leader. In addition, your strategy should include a sense of job ownership for these informal groups. The feeling that "it's our baby" will also be a motivating force to accomplish work. When you instill this sense of ownership in work groups, your employees will want to produce results at a cost acceptable to your organization.

Another way to promote motivation is to organize the work place so that workers can congregate and exchange ideas in pleasant surroundings. Some companies have found that placing the cafeteria facility where the view is best has been a positive motivating force.

4. Motivate Through Praise and Recognition.

I hear it over and over again: "My boss doesn't appreciate what I do, so I'll do just enough to get by." If you are going to be a high-performance individual, it's imperative that you recognize the needs and drives of your people. A deep need of people is to be appreciated. However, despite this obvious need, managers and supervisors constantly fail to let people know they are appreciated. When was the last time your boss told you that your work was appreciated? Or when was the last time you told your spouse that you appreciated all that he or she has done for you? I rest my case. People need to hear words of praise and recognition. It makes them feel valued. This is especially true for younger workers, who have difficulty distinguishing their true value from their doing value. When I ask managers or supervisors why they don't praise or recognize their subordinates for work well done, many older managers have told me: "Why should I? After all, that's what they are getting paid for." Or they have said, "I just don't feel comfortable doing so."

Modern managers must realize that it takes more than money to motivate people. It also takes words of appreciation. Praise costs nothing, and the return is great. Therefore, it should be recognized that one of the best motivational forces in handling people is praising them—particularly in their anxiety-causing areas. You should give praise when a person is trying to do a good job and when a person needs some incentive in order to make progress. Of course, you have to be sincere, as false praise will be seen through. Don't overdo praise, either.

Your strategy is to create a praise and recognition plan for your employees. Praise and recognition can be given by appropriate "chats," "pats on the back," memos, raises and choices of assignments. When you are genuinely concerned about your employees and give them the appreciation they deserve, they will respond with the accomplishment of results.

Motivating your people is a lot like managing your marriage. The more you respect, praise, compliment and encourage your employees, the more productive and satisfying the relationship will be. On the other hand, the more you belittle the self-image of your employees, the more likely it will be for you to have an unproductive and dissatisfying relationship. High-performance managers and supervisors believe in their people. They look at the positives and attempt to minimize the negatives.

Make people feel important for their job accomplishments. Give them the praise and recognition they deserve. These are basic human needs.

5. Motivate Through Positive Performance Feedback.

One of the most important tools in motivating employees is the giving of feedback. Feedback provides an opportunity for employees to see the consequences of their behavior and sets the state for training and development activities. It's a well-researched fact that achievers constantly need to know how well they are doing. Feedback enables high performers to assess their strengths and weaknesses relative to particular projects or activities.

Employees usually will do a good job for you when they know what is expected of them. When you provide this performance feedback and let people know where they stand in a fair and consistent manner, performance will reach higher levels. However, in motivating people through performance feedback it's important that you focus the feedback on behavior and not individual traits of people. A colleague once gave me a hint: Focus on behavior by thinking about adverbs, which relate to behavior actions, rather than adjectives, which relate to traits. So you would say that an individual talked at great length rather than that the person is a big mouth.

Managers should influence employee behavior by providing feedback that preserves and enhances the individual's self-concept. By focusing feedback on observations rather than inferences, you are minimizing the threat to a person's self-worth. If you are able to supply positive feedback, you are developing a long-run strategy of building up confidence within that person. This sense of confidence will also be a self-motivating mechanism. Of course, negative feedback will also be warranted at times. In these situations, you are trying to decrease the likelihood of undesirable behavior.

Positive feedback motivates the employee to gain rewards, while negative feedback can motivate an employee to avoid undesirable consequences. In the long run, it's positive feedback that gets results.

Your strategy then is to encourage two-way feedback between yourself and your employees. Ask your employees how they can improve product or service quality and their job. This feedback will enable you to influence their behavior in a measurable and observable way, which will lead to higher productivity for your organization. It also increases the likelihood that desired behavior will be repeated in the future.

6. Motivate Through Participative Management.

Participative management is primarily a process of creating a climate for subordinates to release their potential for innovation and for constructive suggestions. In practice, this usually means that employees are given an opportunity to participate in various decisions that will affect them directly or indirectly.

An increasing number of managers and supervisors are beginning to recognize that it is profitable to use a participative approach that allows self-motivation. Permitting input from subordinates often requires an attitude change on the part of many managers. It's much easier to tell people what to do than ask them their opinion. Under time pressure, and when you have the necessary information, a direct telling approach will probably be the right strategy. However, managers must realize that employees come with heads in addition to a pair of hands. By allowing employees to give their own suggestions relative to assigned work, policies and procedures, you will tap a hidden source of innovation and motivation. Participative management encourages this self-motivation and enables the work itself to be a source of motivation.

Your strategy is to conduct participative meetings and ask your subordinates to discuss ways they can design and put more challenge into their jobs. It must also be realized that participative management is not permissive management. Your responsibility as manager is to see that the employee is capable of the new challenge and that he or she will receive satisfaction with the job change.

People have different interests and needs, and they should be given an opportunity to grow and develop in their own ways. Participative management is a tool to accomplish this objective.

7. Motivate Through Performance Standards and Performance Reviews.

One of the first steps in improving performance in any organization involves defining and establishing measurable performance standards. Without standards (which should be as clear and specific as par on a golf course), employees have little idea of what is expected of them. And without standards, a manager cannot judge whether or not the quantity or quality of production is appropriate.

Many organizations have difficulty in setting standards. When they do set standards, they generally place too much emphasis on quantity of work in contrast to quality of work. Often this leads workers to assume that quality workmanship is not encouraged or rewarded. Consequently, in setting standards you want to at least think about setting quantity and quality standards. A brainstorming session will prove to you that you can measure quality characteristics. In addition, quality standards will not necessarily mean lower quantity output.

In performance reviews, you provide in a regular and consistent manner the feedback necessary to let people know where they stand. Your basic purpose in these meetings is to make your people aware that you are there to help them improve on their performance.

Your strategy is to jointly set measurable quantity and quality standards and reward employees in relation to the profit payoff from their actions. The strategy of giving rewards for desired behavior will direct your employees into the most efficient and effective way of doing things. Your people deserve to know what target they are shooting at and what rewards they will receive for being on target. Setting performance standards and conducting performance reviews will generate a motivating climate for people to meet their individual and organizational goals.

8. Understand Your Employees' Motivation Profiles.

David C. McClelland is a hero of mine for his insights in applying behavioral science to the motivation of people. In my opinion, his book *The Achieving Society* is one every manager and supervisor should read. McClelland's many years of quantitative research on psychological factors has lead him to believe that the need for achievement is responsible for the economic growth or decline of countries and businesses. Consequently, when we learn not to hold back our achievers, we will have highly productive departments. Unfortunately, many managers and supervisors don't recognize this motivation profile because they are not looking for it.

High achievers are those individuals who will take calculated or moderate risks. They receive little satisfaction from accomplishing easy goals or objectives. You will recognize them because they will ask you, "How am I doing?" They need this feedback because advancement in their career path is important to them. They have an attitude that says, "Here's what I can accomplish if you let me." Recognize these characteristics and give these people some freedom to fly.

McClelland also informs us of two other motivation profiles: the need for power and the need for affiliation. You can easily recognize individuals who have a need for power.

They like to have their ideas predominate, and they really enjoy strongly influencing people and projects. The affiliation-motivated individual wants to be popular and well thought of. In addition, this person sincerely wants to help others but must be in a work environment where there are many opportunities for friendly interpersonal relations.

Operationally, this means that we can best motivate by recognizing each individual's major motivation profile and placing each person in the proper type of job in our organization.

KEYS TO EMPLOYEE MOTIVATION:
A Practical Approach

1. You motivate your employees through their *values*.
2. Your employees want to be proud of you. They want to be a part of a winning team. Your *leadership* style is a major force influencing motivated employee behavior. Do you use a consultative or participative approach, or do you dictate to people?
3. Realize that behavior can be engineered or changed by *positive reinforcement*.
4. Let employees know how well they are doing in meeting company objectives by giving genuine *praise, recognition*, and *performance feedback*.
5. Understand that a person is not like an elevator, he/she is more like a piano. You must learn how to read the music.
6. Encourage employee imput via a planning and/or management-by-commitment system.
7. Set high standards of integrity.
8. Realize that the job content is a strong motivation especially for younger employees.
9. Get the new employee off to a good start.

A final positive motivating thought: Your employees are only what you think they are.

They become only what you think they can become.

ACTION EXERCISE

1. List what motivates *you*.

2. List what you think motivates your employees in general.

3. List three things you could do for those employees who mainly seek *security*.

4. List those things you can do for those employees who mainly seek *self-esteem*.

5. List three things you can do for those employees that have *high-achievement needs*.

ACTION STEP
5

How to Improve Your Communication Effectiveness

To communicate is to live.

—GEORGE DORAN

There's a story told in the book *The Palace Guard*, by Dan Rather and Paul Gates, about a presidential communication problem. President Nixon was working late in a hotel and ordered an aide, "Get me coffee." Since it was late at night, it took some time to call in the hotel personnel and brew a fresh pot. Throughout this time the President kept asking for coffee. It wasn't until the carafe of coffee arrived that it was realized that Nixon wanted an assistant whose name was Coffee.

There's another well-known story, reported in the magazine *Advertising Age*, concerning Coca-Cola's advertising theme "Coke adds life." The senior management of Coca-Cola was very concerned about declining sales of their product in a few Asian markets. It wasn't until they realized that the theme "Coke adds life" had been translated into "Coke brings you back from the dead" were they able to take corrective action. If the President and a worldwide company have communication problems, it's no surprise that for managers and supervisors communications will be the weak link in dealing with people.

Many managers spend approximately 50 percent of their time communicating. Looked at from a different perspective, this means that approximately 50 percent of their salary is allocated to their communication ability. Unfortunately, too many managers don't realize that they have a communication problem. They assume, sometimes wrongly, that they are good communicators because they have been communicating all of their lives.

WHAT IS COMMUNICATION?

Your ability to communicate will be a key skill in your success. It's a skill you can never learn completely. Simply put, communication is nothing more than achieving understanding. It's a process of conveying your thoughts accurately to your listeners. More formally stated, it is a process by which a verbal or nonverbal effort is made by a sender (source) to transmit a message through some channel to establish a commonness with a receiver for the objective of influencing the behavior of the receiver.

The key to communication is understanding. All of us share different experiences, values, attitudes, perceptions and verbal efficiency. Consequently, we don't want to fall into the Humpty Dumpty trap. In Lewis Carroll's classic work *Through the Looking Glass*, Humpty Dumpty said with a bit of arrogance to Alice, "When I use a word, it means just what I choose it to mean, neither more nor less." Don't assume that just because you spoke, you communicated. Words are abstractions, and symbols can mean different things to different people.

So, in defining communication, we are referring to a joining of information and knowledge, to a sharing and understanding in a social process.

In communicating we exchange information so that we achieve an understanding between two or more people. This understanding can be delineated as a set of circles.

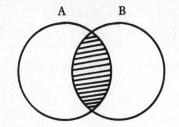

Circle A = understanding exclusive to Person A.
Circle B = understanding exclusive to Person B.

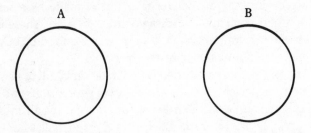

= area of commonness or understanding.

If no communication takes place, there is no commonness. Pictorially, this can be presented in the following way:

ROLES OF COMMUNICATION

Although communication has persuasive application in all management areas, it is particularly important in directing people. As managers, we want to effect change and influence action. In order for you to accomplish this you must be able to communicate your plans, coordinate work and assign work so that all departments are heading in the same direction. In addition, you must attract the best qualified people into your organization, which requires interview communication skills. All of these functions and activities require the transfer of information in a clear and precise fashion. Your message cannot be delivered in a vague or murky way. Too often we speak before we think, and consequently the wrong word or phrase is spoken to the audience we are trying to influence.

We must be aware that we can strongly influence employee productivity just by the way we say "hi" in the morning. The nonverbal enthusiasm or lack of it helps set the stage for the work output that day and other days. Some managers and supervisors believe that they have to belittle their workers with harsh words to get them to work harder. This negative communication style almost always results over the long run in less productivity and more fire-fighting activity.

In addition to the directing and influencing purposes of communication, managers and supervisors should be aware that another major purpose of communication is to exchange information. Communication is not a one-way street. Rensis Likert, in his book *New Patterns of Management*, mentions a study conducted at a public-utility company. There only 50 percent of an employee group felt free to discuss job concerns with their respective bosses. Apparently, these managers didn't communicate as well as they thought they did.

Another role of communication is to make better decisions. Unfortunately, many managers must rely on information that is passed through second- and third-hand sources. Thus, as your organization grows, problems of transmission and reception of information multiply at a geometric rate. As managers and supervisors improve their communication skills on all levels, improved decision making results.

THE COMMUNICATION SYSTEM

In the broadest sense, the purpose of communication is to influence positive action and behavior. Without good communication you and your subordinates cannot work well together in developing and achieving organizational goals and objectives. Although we want action, many managers and supervisors fail to communicate because they don't realize how complicated the communication process actually is. In fact, we really communicate a lot less than we think. We must recognize that taking communication for granted only increases the probability of not communicating. Communication is really a complex system of interrelated parts. An understanding of each part is crucial in getting your ideas and thoughts across to another person. Therefore, let's look at what we call communication in a piecemeal fashion. When you understand the communication system model, and where communication can go wrong, you will be a better communicator.

THE COMMUNICATION SYSTEM MODEL

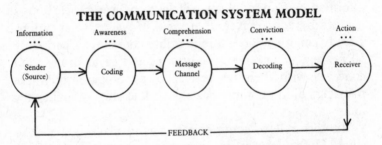

Noise (•••) is anything (psychological or physical) that interferes with or reduces the effectiveness of the communication process.

The communication model indicates potential breakdown points: (1) source/sender perception problems; (2) coding word/symbol problems; (3) accuracy/message-channel problems; (4) decoding words/symbols; (5) receiver/listening perception problems; (6) feedback/nonverbal inference problems.

For communication to be effective you need a sender and a receiver. Communication begins with the sender formulating some ideas or thoughts to be communicated. The idea may be to find ways to increase productivity, or to change some policy. However, we all have different education levels, experiences and expectancies. Therefore, we must realize that our perceptions of reality are going to influence how we communicate. Understanding the adage "As we perceive, so shall we communicate" is a first step in understanding good communications. We all have different perceptions. Consequently, if we want to improve our communication skills, we must put ourselves in the shoes of the receiver.

English is a phonetic language, meaning it is formed by sounds. The sender must, therefore, code the proper meaning into abstractions, words, gestures or pictures. This coding process transforms the idea into a message. In this second step, you must be like a good marketing individual; you must package your product in such a way that the receiver finds it attractive and understandable.

The message channel could be various forms of media, the telephone, speaking or writing. You must make sure that the message channel chosen is related to the idea you want to get across. If an individual is to receive a raise in salary, you shouldn't let the pay envelope inform that person. Telling the person directly how proud you are and how you appreciate his or her efforts is a much better approach. A formal letter of praise would also be a good follow-up. It's useful to realize that many times it's not what we say or give but how we say or give it that is important.

In the decoding process, the receiver must translate the sender's message into internal thoughts. The symbols, words or gestures chosen must have the same or approximately the same meaning for both parties. In other words, communication is facilitated when the common experience of the sender and receiver meet about the message.

Too often managers and supervisors become irate when there is a misunderstanding of the message. They believe they spoke in unambiguous terms. Their problem is that

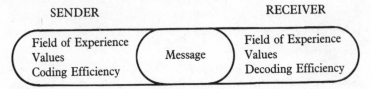

they forgot to ask for feedback. This reverse communication role requires the sender now to be an active listener. Managers and supervisors must realize that effective communication is always bilateral, not unilateral. You should not assume that whenever you write or speak your message will be understood. Those managers that discourage feedback will not be effective managers.

BARRIERS TO EFFECTIVE COMMUNICATION

Your ability to communicate effectively with people is a key skill in your management arsenal. Communication skills are the foundation for your interpersonal-relationship effectiveness. All managers and supervisors communicate, but few communicate well in a consistent manner. If you are not conscious of the quality of your communication efforts and cognizant of communication barriers, the productivity of your operation or organization will be adversely affected. Therefore, in getting your meaning across you should be knowledgeable in the complexities and barriers in the communication process. Don't assume communication occurs just because you sent a message. What, then, are the barriers to effective communication, and what can managers or supervisors do to more effectively communicate with their people?

1. Perception Problems

Differences in perception, which are largely expectations and environmentally influenced, are a major cause of disagreements between people and departments. People and departments respond not to what is actually happening, but to what they perceive is happening. We all see reality or what we think is reality from our own viewpoint. We perceive fact based on our own particular needs, wants, interests and emotional well-being. Realize that your employees perceive data and information very selectively. Consequently, no two people will respond to or understand your message in exactly the same way. Your message may be received, but it will not necessarily be perceived. Or you may receive a message from someone of a different background and, due to your perception, conclude that the individual is just the emotional type and ignore what is being said. To overcome this barrier, realize that people will only understand part of your message. Consequently, it's your responsibility to take perceptual differences into account when you are coding and transmitting messages or ideas to others. Resist the temptation to form instant perceptions of people based solely on their physical appearance or educational background. Encourage feedback so that you and the receiver feel confident that you both have achieved a commonness, or an understanding of the idea.

2. Distortion of Message

Distortion is a phenomenon that occurs when we communicate what we think we heard. Often we or our subordinates don't feel free to question the meaning of communication coming from above. Consequently, we tend to add or subtract information. An interesting example of this tendency is illustrated by the following formal communication. A West Point friend and officer supplied me with this story written by an unknown source:

FORMAL COMMUNICATION IN AN ORGANIZATION

A colonel issued the following directive to the executive officer:

Tomorrow evening at approximately 2000 hours, Halley's Comet will be visible in this area, an event which occurs only once every 75 years. Have the men to fall out in the battalion area in fatigues, and I will explain this rare phenomenon to them. In case of rain, we will not be able to see anything, so assemble the men in the theater and I will show films of it.

EXECUTIVE OFFICER TO THE COMPANY COMMANDER:

By order of the colonel, tomorrow at 2000 hours, Halley's Comet will appear above the battalion area. If it rains, fall the men out in fatigues; then march to the theater where the rare phenomenon will take place, something which occurs once every 75 years.

COMPANY COMMANDER TO LIEUTENANT:

By order of the colonel in fatigues at 2000 hours tomorrow evening, the phenomenal Halley's Comet will appear in the theater. In case of rain in the battalion area, the colonel will give another order, something which occurs once every 75 years.

LIEUTENANT TO SERGEANT:

Tomorrow at 2000 hours, the colonel will appear in the theater with Halley's Comet, something which happens every 75 years. If it rains, the colonel will order the comet into the battalion area.

SERGEANT TO SQUAD:

When it rains tomorrow at 2000 hours, the phenomenal 75-year-old General Halley, accompanied by the colonel, will drive his Comet through the battalion area in his fatigues.

To overcome this barrier, efforts must be made by managers and supervisors not to surround themselves with too many people who can filter the primary source of information. Some communication consultants suggest that no more than three individuals be involved in any communication. Another suggestion is for managers and supervisors to work on developing a trust relationship with their subordinates. Create an environment where subordinates can feel free to question what is not understood.

3. Values, Attitudes and Temperament Differences

We are all mixtures of different values, attitudes and temperaments. We have different likes, dislikes, strengths and weaknesses. These characteristics direct our behavior and reinforce our biases. Consequently, our biases often prevent us from being objective when we communicate. Because of this, we don't communicate the whole of what we expect. Then when we inspect employees' work, it reaffirms our prejudices that these people are incompetent.

Attitudes and values are important determinants in how people work and respond to changes. By communicating within the context of individual attitudes and values, we can positively influence individual behavior and performance. Therefore, to overcome attitudes and values barriers, managers and supervisors must increase their effectiveness in the communication skill of empathy. We can show our empathy by choosing our words very carefully in terms of another's interest, likes and dislikes. Another suggestion is to take the word "I" out of your vocabulary and replace it with the word "you." When we show our concern for the feelings of others, we are more likely to be listened to. This develops communication between people and encourages a better utilization of the feedback link in our communication system model. Tolerate, and try to understand the differences in values and attitudes among your employees.

4. Verbal and Nonverbal Language Barriers

We are aware that words mean different things to different people. The word "tip" to a stock speculator means insider's information, to a waiter or waitress it means extra income. Semanticists have concluded that there are over 10,000 meanings for 400 common words. It comes as no surprise, then, that people can go their separate directions, each believing they each know what was intended. The same word may have different emotional meanings in different parts of the country or different meanings with different age groups. "Hierarchy" may be a good personnel-management word, but it could be void of meaning in another group situation. To help prevent misunderstanding, managers and supervisors should choose their words very carefully when talking to different groups. You must be conscious of the fact that there are different levels in the management triangle and, therefore, different concerns and perceptions. Choose your words and illustrations carefully.

Professional poker players often wear dark glasses. They have learned that they have communicated in nonverbal forms. The dilated pupil was a signal or clue that the poker player had a good hand. The raised eyebrow communicated disbelief in getting such a crummy hand. There are many other nonverbal clues that communicate more loudly than our words. The way you dress in front of groups speaks volumes about you. Are your arms folded when you speak to your people, telling them that you have a closed mind or attitude? Do you look at the ceiling when people talk to you? You're telling them that you don't care what they are talking about.

To overcome these verbal barriers watch your technical, academic or trade vocabulary when you are speaking. When you go to your doctor, do you want him to use his medical-school language on you, or do you want him to explain things in layman's language? Have the same consideration for your people and other groups you come in contact with. As for nonverbal communication, be more cognizant of the reaction of people to your gestures, tilted posture, dress, etc. Your nonverbal communication will likely increase, decrease or erase your verbal communications. To miss the nonverbal communication of your subordinates is to miss a major part of their message.

5. Confusing Inferences/Implications and Facts

We communicate at least in two dimensions, i.e., what is said and what is implied or inferred. Therefore, what you say or what the listener receives can be two different messages. You may say to your boss or subordinate that your department needs a change in design. Your boss may interpret that to mean that you are saying he has an inefficient organization or operation. Your subordinates may believe that you want to make major changes. You may only be thinking about a minor change in paper flow.

Be careful of the emotional association that words have. As a manager or supervisor your failure to recognize the multi-level dimension to our communication will result in inefficient communication and lower company profits. To overcome this barrier, train yourself to listen to what is meant rather than what is said. Listen to the ideas as opposed to the facts.

6. Not Thinking Before Talking or Writing

How many of you have suffered from foot-in-the-mouth disease? Once you say something, you cannot get it back. Thinking is nothing more than planning and packaging your thoughts before you transmit your message. It's one communication skill that most of us need help on. Always clarify in your mind's eye what you have to say before you say or write it.

You must first be able to communicate an idea or thought to yourself before you communicate it to anyone else. Before you write a memo or a report decide on your overall purpose, and let people know your purpose rather than have them guess at it or find it out at the end of the memo or report. As your writing becomes clearer, your effectiveness will increase. Therefore, in overcoming this barrier we must learn how to become more concise and precise. Many of us tend to use a lot of words when a few would do. In your speaking and writing attempt to produce good music; cut out all that interferes with a well-orchestrated piece.

7. Failure to Listen

Perhaps the biggest barrier to effective communication is our failure to listen. Research studies have shown that most managers and supervisors listen with only 25 to 50 percent efficiency. This means that 50 to 75 percent of what we listen to is never processed. We all have a tendency of talking too much and listening too little. It is also a well-researched fact that, on average, we speak at a rate of 150 words per minute but that our minds can process at a rate of 500 to 600 words per minute. This rate of approximately 3.7 to 1 is the reason why we mentally wander while people speak, and consequently we don't pay full attention to the speaker. This usually results in not grasping the critical components of messages. Consequently, tasks are not always performed correctly and objectives are not met in the appropriate time frame.

Good listening isn't easy, but when managers and supervisors learn to listen properly they will find a payoff for themselves. To help us overcome this barrier here are a few ideas for you to consider. (1) Learn to get ready to listen. Resolve to give your full attention to the speaker both mentally and nonverbally. (2) Listen actively. Since we can think three to four times faster than we talk, use your thinking capacity to become a better listener. Try to empathize with the speaker and focus on the idea of what is being said. (3) Practice feedback. Question or paraphrase what was being said. Try to learn more about the message or instruction communicated.

8. Jumping to Decisions Too Quickly

Sometimes we think we know what a speaker is going to say, and we just listen with one ear. We reach a conclusion based on our preconceived idea of what the facts are. A humorous story—source unknown—illustrates this point (this tendency to jump to a decision quickly can be disastrous in real life):

> A Marine Corps general was visiting an installation and asked to see the bugler privately. "Can you play fire call?" he inquired.
>
> "Yes sir," replied the marine.
>
> "Then meet me tomorrow at 5:00 A.M. in front of the post headquarters and don't mention this to anyone," said the general.
>
> The post commander was so eager to know what was going on that he pressured the bugler into telling him about his conversation with the general. That night the post's fire station was a beehive of activity as equipment was washed and polished. Even the door hinges were oiled. The next morning the marine bugler reported to the general.
>
> "Sound church call," the general ordered.
>
> "But, sir, you asked me if I knew fire call."
>
> "Yes, son, I know, but now please play church call."
>
> As the first notes pierced the early morning stillness, the doors of the fire station flew open and out roared the trucks with bells clanging and sirens screaming.

How can you overcome this tendency to jump to decisions too quickly? Learn to listen with two ears. Don't let your emotions make you deaf because someone brings up a topic that is controversial, or because you think you have all the answers. Listen with patience until you have given everyone a fair amount of time to explain their point of view. Good leaders have learned to be good listeners. Based on all the data and information you received, make your decision. When managers and supervisors jump to decisions too quickly by hearing but not listening, it could mean the difference between profit and loss.

TIPS AND STRATEGIES FOR IMPROVING YOUR COMMUNICATION EFFECTIVENESS

1. Management consultant John Morris tells us in *Make Yourself Clear* (McGraw-Hill, 1972) that the basic principles for using words well, whether in writing or speaking, may be conveniently grouped under five guidelines:

    (a) Be brief—cut out useless words.
    (b) Be simple—avoid gobbledygook and pompous polysyllables.
    (c) Be direct—use strong, active verbs and normal sentence order.
    (d) Be clear—be sure your audience understands your words.
    (e) Be human—communicate with people.

2. Semanticist S. I. Hayakawa has said that in any conversation between two people there are really four messages present. What you say, what you mean, what the receiver hears and what the receiver thinks he hears. Realize that your ability to communicate is linked by your perception of yourself and the receiver's perception of himself or herself.

3. Be aware of the complexity of communication. Like golf, it is a lot harder than it looks. Any number of things can go wrong in golf, and this is also true in the symbolic/abstract

communication process. If you are conscious of the fact that you need to improve your communication skills, you will be on the road to improving these skills.

4. Some women state that men cannot communicate their feelings and, therefore, it is possible to misread what is being said. Some men state that women don't say what they mean and, therefore, it is again possible to misread what is being said. It could be at this moment in time that men are more external (speak from the school of hard knocks) and women are more internal (speak more from their feelings to get their point across). Be aware of possible sex differences in communicating, and become more of an active listener.

5. Smile, be enthusiastic, look people in the eye when you are talking to them. In other words, give them your full attention. Don't give listeners the impression that what you have to say is more important. They will mentally shut you off. Remember it takes a sender and a receiver for effective communication to take place.

6. Listen for the "what" and "why" of what is being said. You want to be tuned into the total meaning of what is transmitted to you. Be conscious of the nonverbal communication operating and the motivation behind the source.

7. Watch your words. Don't use your technical language when speaking to a general audience. They will not be impressed. You must tailor your words and message to your specific audience.

8. Be positive in your communication. Let people know what you expect, but praise them when they do a good job. Through positive communication you build confidence in your people, and this will result in a good working attitude. Negative communication only reinforces a negative self-concept and, rather than increasing productivity, actually makes it worse.

9. Paraphrase and ask questions. When you want to make sure your message was understood, ask the receiver to paraphrase your message. Then through the use of a few questions you will know whether or not your message got across.

10. Hold at least one weekly meeting with your key people. You want to communicate your ideas in a proper environment at

the proper time. Something you say on the run will not have the impact of a formal meeting. Therefore, always consider the place and employees' frame of mind when delivering your message.

11. Tell people what you are going to tell them\before you tell them. It reduces stress (psychological noise). People will be less apt to make inferences on what is coming, and consequently better communication will result.

12. Make use of a bulletin board for coming events. You know what is coming so don't surprise your people on coming events. Your employees don't want to hear about what is going on inside their organization from someone outside the organization.

13. Take steps to improve your credibility and trust level. If you practice open communication and deal fairly and ethically with your employees, your message will get through. When we don't trust people, we don't really listen to them.

14. Occasionally hold a breakfast meeting with your people. In a relaxed environment away from the office you will see people as they really are. Generalizations about people will tend to evaporate, and communication will improve.

15. Don't argue. Make a genuine attempt to see the other person's point of view. By arguing you will only bring out the negative defense mechanism in people. Communication is lost at this point.

16. Don't overdo it. Don't fall in love with your own voice. It's possible to give and say too much. People may remember the verbosity and forget your message.

17. Realize that you will never learn enough about communications.

Communication has been a problem since the beginning of time. However, the more you are aware of why communication can go wrong and what you can do about it, the more effective you will be as a communicator. Remember Ralph Waldo Emerson's words, "It's a luxury to be understood." Keep working at it.

ACTION EXERCISE

Paraphrasing/feedback is essential to the communication process. However, don't think of paraphrasing as simply stating the other person's message in a different way. Paraphrasing/feedback is really a way of revealing your understanding of the signals sent. Don't be caught in the trap of telling a subordinate that his report is bad when you really mean that the reproduction is bad. Without paraphrasing/feedback both of you would walk away with completely different understandings. Develop a training program to improve the effectiveness of communications within your shop.

ACTION STEP
6

How to Recruit and Select the Best People

The most valuable of all capital is that invested in human beings.
—ALFRED MARSHALL

Recruiting and selecting the right person in the right job at the right time is a lot like a marriage relationship. It takes good communication, careful evaluation of your needs, selection from the best sources, strategy, listening skills and, yes, luck. This process of recruiting and selecting the right people for your operation is not an easy task, but planning will be your key to successful recruiting and deciding which individuals are most likely to perform best for you. Your skill in obtaining the best people for your department or company will be one—if not the number-one—critical factor in your success and the continued growth of your organization. You are only as good as your employees.

In some organizations, employee turnover runs as high as 40 percent per year. In smaller businesses a figure of 25 percent is not uncommon. Career researchers have reported that today the average person changes jobs seven times in a lifetime. One major reason for such a high job turnover among individuals is the fact that many managers, supervisors and others hire without a clear idea of what they are looking for. Divorces can be expensive and unpleasant. It is a waste of your time and money to hire someone and then lose that person within a short time interval either due to overselling the job or because the applicant didn't understand the company and/or the job. With this in mind, this chapter is designed, first, to present methods that will help you recruit or search for those candidates best suited to your operations and, second, to develop interview skills to help you select the best.

HOW TO RECRUIT THE RIGHT PERSON FOR THE JOB

Proper recruiting methods or strategies are crucial to the continued growth and success of your organization. The most common recruiting failure is not taking the time to evaluate the real needs of your operation or organization before deciding to hire a new employee. Even though the recruitment of competent people is clearly one of your most important decisions, most managers and supervisors lack a recruiting system. This lack of a system usually results in taking more of your time interviewing applicants who do not meet your standards and generally results in not hiring the best candidate for your situation. Still another common mistake is the hiring of a person who can do "anything," or hiring a person who is an employee's "friend." This attitude or philosophy has led to the demise of many businesses. Intuition cannot replace a system that will identify manpower needs and include a process to obtain the necessary talent for your operation. Nevertheless, your intuition can be a helpful decision-making process when the facts have surfaced in a particular situation. With these thoughts in mind, the recruiting process can be summarized in a few steps:

1. Assess Manpower Requirements.

In today's fast-paced world, managers and supervisors can no longer wait to think about their management needs until the time that someone retires, dies or leaves for any reason. You cannot be passive and assume that people with the proper skills will appear at your door when you need them. In addition, as a result of federal and state affirmative-action programs, some managers and supervisors must recruit women and minorities into their organizations. Consequently, managers and supervisors must assess their situation, develop company and department goals and strategies, then determine their future management requirements.

In the assessment process, it's a good idea to ask yourself the following question: What is the forecast demand for our product or service? As we move out of a recession, do we add temporary help or full-time help? Given the nature of this demand, what kinds of skills, attitudes and abilities are required? What impact will the changing environment have upon our operation? What is our break-even point? At what point will hiring an additional employee add more to our costs than our profits? What budget constraints exist? What impact will new technology have? What interest or rate of inflation can be expected?

Be honest and realistic with your thoughts.

2. Determine Job Requirements.

Many words have been written describing how to determine job requirements. However, from my experience, it all boils down to asking yourself three basic questions: What will the employee do? How will the employee do it? Why does this employee do this work?

To determine job requirements, just sit down with a yellow pad of paper and simply think about and jot your ideas down on these questions. When you do this type of study, it is important for you to think about the job requirements rather than the person currently filling the position. The individual currently performing the work may be too overqualified for the requirements of the job. When you have completed this step, the objective of improving your recruitment methods will have greatly improved.

3. Develop a Job Description.

Once you have determined job requirements, your next step is to develop a job description. Traditionally, a job description summarizes pertinent facts about a particular job. It gives the job title, a general description on the work performed, duties, responsibilities and occasionally relationships of this specific job to other jobs. An advantage of this type of job description is that it does enable you to develop an employee-orientation program, and it can be a basis for supervisory control and disciplinary action if required. The development of job descriptions is also a good way to prevent disputes as to which individual is supposed to do what work. From my experience, the one problem with the traditional job description is that the focus is on the job, not on the accountabilities of the manager or supervisor in the job. In a job description, the responsibilities and duties will establish the fence within which managers and supervisors direct their operations. However, the accountability addition to a job description will later serve performance-evaluation purposes.

4. Determine Personal Requirements and Working Conditions.

The next step in developing a recruitment process for yourself is to think about the personal qualifications of the individual and understand the employee working conditions. The chemistry must be right between you and the new employee. What attitude(s), what work experiences, what physical and mental requirements, what skills and what education are necessary for the job (to make that chemistry right)? In addition to determining the proper personal requirements, develop an understanding of the environmental conditions under which this employee must work. Is there a hazardous gaseous or dust environment? Or is the risk that of a paper cut in reshuffling paper?

RECRUITMENT SOURCES

There are many recruitment sources, and there are many opinions as to which is best. Which is best will usually vary with the type of position to be filled. Managers and supervisors, therefore, should be familiar with and utilize several recruitment sources. If your needs run from clerical, secretarial, semi-skilled, machine operators to hi-tech people and upper-division level, your sources will vary from employment agencies to executive recruiters.

Your recruiting sources include your own organization, public and private employment agencies, classified or other advertisements, search firms, industry organizations, colleges and universities, trade schools, unsolicated applications, labor unions and referrals. I've found that many managers, supervisors and business owners often limit themselves to two sources: within the company and within the industry. Within the industry can mean "pirating" from other companies. This approach has cost and time advantages and can be the best recruitment decision. Nevertheless, from an overall viewpoint, my experience tells me that when companies occasionally go outside to obtain the necessary skills needed, they will be a more profitable company. They may be uncomfortable at first, but fresh and different viewpoints can make your operation a growing one. However, more managers and supervisors seem to agree to first look inside their own organization. Recruiting from within will be less costly and should have motivational benefits for other employees. For small firms, a promotion-from-within policy can often offset the wage/salary disparity between small and large business.

Employment agencies, another alternative for you, are state-licensed placement services. They can perform a valuable service for the manager or supervisor who is frustrated by a job search. You can have the protection of anonymity and let the agency do a significant part of the work. Fees for the applicant usually range from 10 to 15 percent of gross annual earnings. Agencies deal with large numbers of clerical and semi-skilled workers. Consequently their knowledge about the candidates and your company will be limited. A "near fit" seems to be the rule of thumb in many employment agencies. Historically, agencies have not performed well in upper-income levels due to their high volume business.

Executive-search, professional-recruitment firms, or "head hunters," as they are usually called, are not placement services. Executive-search firms are usually not licensed, since no contract is signed between the firm and the candidate. Unlike agencies, search firms work for your company, not for individuals. Their fees will vary in different economic conditions, but usually they seek up to one third of the candidate's annual salary. There are contingency-search firms, retainer-search firms and time-and-expense search firms. When a contingency firm accepts a search assignment, your company only pays when the candidate is delivered. The disadvantage is that you may receive no results depending upon the out-of-pocket expenses anticipated by the search firms.

A retainer firm's usual arrangement is to receive a one-third fee in advance, one third at the end of 60 or 90 days and one third due when the candidate is hired. If no candidate is hired, the first one third is not received. With this alternative, your firm will usually receive excellent service. However, some companies feel uncomfortable for paying in advance for some unknown quantity.

The third alternative is where you set a budget in terms of time and expense. The advantage, of course, is that you set the budget. But once the budget limit is reached, you may not have your candidate.

In the final analysis, the broader your search, the better your chances of recruiting the right person in the right job at the right time. Of course, cost-benefit analysis is assured to apply in your recruiting methods.

SELECTING THE BEST CANDIDATES

Your productivity and profitability depend in large part on your selection decision. Of all the decisions you make, probably nothing will have such a major impact on your day-to-day activities and income statement as your selection decision. Your subordinates will be most influential in your success and the success of your company.

Not knowing how to conduct an employee interview can be very expensive. Even in favorable employer economic situations, when a large labor pool is available, the manager or supervisor must still select the candidate who best meets the requirements of the job.

PREPARE FOR THE INTERVIEW

Many businesses and other organizations (military, police, city, government) are operated by people with high technical skills and low management skills. Consequently, an interview process, while sorely needed, is usually nonexistent. The manager does the interviewing between jobs or meetings and often sees the selection of personnel as a necessary but nuisance-causing interruption in the productive day. With this approach and attitude it's no surprise that the process is riddled with mistakes, and often the best candidate isn't selected.

Probably, the biggest mistake that business managers or supervisors make is to play the interview by ear. They don't organize all the necessary data about the candidate or the company, make a list of key questions or take the time out to prepare the physical setting. Even the most skilled interviewer needs to have some preplanning questions to insure the covering of key areas. You must also prepare to avoid discrimination charges. Most discrimination is not intentional in the sense that you will willfully discriminate. However, the fact is you may not have intended to, but the outcome is the same. Illegal discrimination can be based on: race, color, sex, religion, national origin, age, weight, handicap, marital status or Vietnam veteran status. Your questions must be occupation related. An off-the-cuff question may open up your organization to a lawsuit. Stick with the job-qualifications questions and show an interest in the person you are interviewing.

THE INTERVIEW PROCESS

Opening Up the Interview

In preparing for the interview, you received the individual's application form, resume and/or other documents. Break the ice by thanking the person for taking time out to talk with you, and discuss some item of the applicant's personal interest. You might say, for example, "I see from your resume that you enjoy tennis [bowling, and so on]." Your objective at this point is to get the interviewee to feel at ease and talk freely. You want to create a positive communication climate. By reviewing the application form and resume you can come up with questions that are easy to answer, nonthreatening and encouraging.

The Semi-Structured Interview

A semi-structured interview will be your key for a successful interview process. Practical experience has demonstrated that it offers the highest probability of obtaining the right candidate for the job. Without such an approach, bias factors tend to be higher, gaps in comparable information will exist and omission of relevant information will develop.

Basically, a semi-structured, or pattern, interview is a procedure whereby each interviewee is asked the same question in the same order within a particular time frame. It doesn't mean that you cannot ask other questions, but it does provide a set of comparable answers and information on each individual. The semi-structured interview will give you control over the actual interview and result in the selection of competent and qualified employees. Structured questions are those questions that you or your staff have determined beforehand based on job qualifications. Your secondary questions will require you to be an active listener so that you can encourage the interviewee to enlarge on answers given.

A good plan is to group your easy questions first and then group those that require more thinking. Your first set of questions should be broad or general and give no indication as to the qualification being measured or sought. Questions such as:

1. How is your tennis coming along?
2. How did you hear about XYZ Company?
3. What interested you in XYZ Company?
4. What do you consider some of your most important skills (or, what do you consider to be your strengths)?
5. What do you want to be doing one year (five years) from now?
6. What were some of your responsibilities in your past jobs?
7. What did you particularly like or excel in?

Be careful not to ask questions that have a simple yes or no answer.

Now, to insure that each interviewee is asked the same job-related questions, you move into your structured questions. It's a good idea to take notes during the interview, but explain to the interviewee that you will be doing so and explain why. Ask at least two questions per qualification criterion. One question should be directed to a past experience on the job, e.g., can you give me an example of how you...? The second question should be present or problem-situation oriented, e.g., which approach would you use in this situation...? Go through this process until you have covered all of the main qualifications for the particular job. During the interview it is important for you not to argue with the interviewee and be an active listener. You should note not only *what* is said and how it is said, but also what is not said. If a person gives a rather long answer, paraphrase what was said to make sure you understand what was being said. If a person gives you too many details about his or her life not relevant to you, remind the person about your time frame.

Concluding the Interview

Near the end of the interview summarize the duties and responsibilities of the job position and let the applicant be given another opportunity to discuss his or her qualifications. The interview is a two-way process, and this is a good time for the applicant to ask questions. You have reached your information objectives, and the applicant wants information to evaluate your company. It is important for the applicant to leave the interview feeling that he or she has had a good opportunity to discuss and express his or her qualifications for the position. You then finish the interview by thanking the applicant for taking the time to come in and, if possible, letting the candidate know when you will probably make a decision.

POST-INTERVIEW PROCESS PROCEDURE

After the interview immediately write up a summary of your impressions of the candidate. Don't leave it to your memory. Your memory will omit some important details. This is especially true for the third to last candidate interviewed. You will want to note some of the candidate's strong and weak points, motivation, attitudes, skills and perhaps some items that are still unresolved in your mind.

In the post-interview process, it is essential for references to be checked. You must decide which individual bosses or supervisors or people who worked with or below the interviewee are most critical for the position. Don't delegate this responsibility. Only you know what needs to be clarified or checked. When you call these people, also ask for others they could recommend who know the applicant. Then summarize their comments.

A position-comparison matrix is a good tool to use. Basically, list the criteria for the position on one axis and the names of the candidates on the other. Then rate each candidate on each criterion.

After this effort has been put forward, the actual selection is almost anticlimatic. As a matter of fact, you probably did such a good job interviewing that you will be very confident in your selection and will be able to give this individual, to a certain extent, a free rein. This means you gain more time with the selection of good people. After you have notified the individual and the person accepts the position, you should inform all other serious candidates that the position is filled.

As a final action exercise, file your semi-structured interview records for at least one year to avoid discrimination charges, say a prayer that you have selected the best and set up an incident file on the new employee.

ACTION EXERCISE

Outline the questions you will want to ask in a semi-structured interview. Write down some introductory questions, and a question that gauges a job candidate's past and present experience for each qualification you are looking for.

ACTION STEP

7

How to Organize Your Organization

Never follow the crowd.
—BERNARD M. BARUCH

A well-tuned organization, like a lean and athletic individual, will move and function smoothly and safely around current problems and future threats. Your organization is the foundation of your efficiency and effectiveness. As such, it is the means by which you organize the human and financial resources at your command to ward off danger and meet your operational and company objectives. Your organization cannot afford to grow fat by serving itself, but must be kept lean, and it must change as conditions change.

There is no substitute for a good organization. A good organization is essential to the success of any profit or non-profit enterprise. A good organization, even with a mediocre product or service, can be profitable and run a better competitive product or service out of the market. A mediocre organization with its inefficiencies and wastes of resources can run good products and services into the ground. Therefore, it is essential that managers, supervisors and business owners make sure that they are properly organized for their particular stage of growth.

One of the first steps in thinking about a better organization is for you to realize that your present organization can be improved. You must have a philosophy of how you can do more with less and less. As such, you should view your present organization not as an end in itself but as a means to an end. You must continually think about how our operation can become more efficient and effective. This is your responsibility. Recall the last time your car was stuck in the snow or mud. By cooperative effort with others all pushing in the same direction, you reached your objective of dislodging the stuck car. A good organization will enable you to achieve results that could not have been achieved as effectively or efficiently through your own individual efforts.

The word "organization" is used with different meanings in management. To some people, "organization" refers to the people who do the work or to the business in total. To others, the word "organization" refers to the senior-management team. Still other organizations refer to arrangements of work activities and tasks through systematic planning. One of the best known definitions on the nature and purpose of organization was stated by management consultant Oliver Sheldon. According to Sheldon, "organization is the process of so combining the work which individuals or groups have to perform with the facilities necessary for its execution, that the duties so performed provide the best channel for the efficient, systematic, positive and coordinated application of the available effort." Although many people, when referring to the organization, are referring to the personnel or the formal organization structure, it should now be clear that the term "organization" embraces a very comprehensive meaning. In improving our skills to learn how to better organize our organization, we now realize that organizing is a dual process. It requires the logical grouping of work activities necessary to obtain results, and it requires the proper assignment of people with the necessary authority and accountability to manage these work activities. More formally stated, organization refers to the activity–authority structure of a business or other organization.

ORGANIZING FOR SUCCESSFUL OPERATIONS

One key to operating an efficient operation is to design your organization around well-defined work activities and tasks. Unfortunately, many managers and supervisors tend to think about organizing their departments around their people. However, successful individuals have discovered that they must first think in terms of present and future work activities before they think about people. Therefore, strickly speaking, your organization design at first does not directly involve people, but focuses on defining activities and grouping these activities to accomplish your planned objectives.

One of your first jobs in organizing your organization is to make a decision on the number and types of positions you will need to satisfy the demands of your markets. Simultaneously, you also decide on the corresponding authorities, responsibilities and accountabilities inherent in each position. Failure to do this will result in overlapping activities, gaps in essential areas and explosive people problems. Perhaps you should think about designing your organization in the same way that an architect would design an efficient office building. You must consider the work to be done, the climate you want to create, energy efficiency, and your customers. In addition, you must provide for growth. If you add offices or positions without an overall strategy, your organization, like the office building, could collapse.

Of course, you must also be concerned with organizing people. How people are organized will influence their productivity, development and accomplishment of organizational goals. However, prior to this, you must decide on what unique combination of human, technical and management skills are required for the created positions that cover the work. A dollar value placed on each position should also be determined at this time. The contribution that each position offers the organization should determine its economic worth. The establishment of written job descriptions and job specifications should also precede the matching of individuals to work positions. Failure to take these preparatory steps will lead to territorial confusion, decreasing productivity and a lower profit level.

In the early stages of a business, and in some cases where the company has existed for many years, this consultant has found no formal reporting relationship. To these organizations I say, hire an office manager, start working on job descriptions, job specifications and a simple organization chart, and assign people to positions where you can make maximum use of their skills.

WHEN SHOULD YOU MAKE ORGANIZATION CHANGES?

As your department, company or market grows, changes in your organization will be required. Managers and supervisors must be alert to the clues that indicate that their organization structure can be improved.

1. Rising Costs.   The cost of your product is a function of the materials and the time taken by your people and machinery to produce and distribute the product to consumers. If the product takes longer to produce, your costs will increase. By taking longer to produce the same product, your efficiency is decreasing; this is a sign that you may have an organization problem.

2. Job Conflict.   If more of your time is taken up settling conflicts among subordinates about who should be doing the task or activity, you need to consider reorganizing some job activities.

3. Too Much Paperwork.   Too much paperwork will result in postponement of decision making. Consequently, the efficiency and effectiveness of your unit will decline.

4. High Turnover.   The turnover rate usually is an important indicator of how employees view their work and supervision. If employees see their work as becoming less meaningful and worthwhile, you will probably experience increasing turnover rates; this is a sign that you should think more seriously about reorganizing work.

5. Failure to Meet Objectives.   When objectives were first set, the parties involved set realistic time schedules. Somewhere along the way in meeting your production, marketing or financial objectives, cooperation broke down. If you are experiencing such delays, chances are you may not be organized properly.

6. Lack of Advancement Opportunities.   How much opportunity is there for careers in your organization? As your unit starts growing, some employees will be ready to assume greater responsibility and authority in your operation.

7. Size of Operation.   No organization should grow larger than one that can be sufficiently understood, controlled and directed by its manager or supervisor. In periods of rapid growth, efforts should be made to determine the proper ratio between a manager's or supervisor's ability and operation complexity.

STEPS TO ORGANIZE YOUR ORGANIZATION

As mentioned before, your organization is the foundation of your efficiency and effectiveness. It is the means by which you will be able to group work activities and resources to make a higher level of profit. Without a well-defined structure, you will be at a major competitive disadvantage. Your job, then, is to design a structure that will coordinate the energies of your people to serve your customers, and change with changes in your strategies. In addition, your job is to communicate to your people why they are organized as they are and why they have certain accountabilities. By clearly thinking ahead as to what positions are necessary both to create demand for your products or services and to service demand, your organizational unit will take a giant step in efficient organization design. Your organization sets the stage for how people are organized, which, in turn, influences how their skills can best be utilized.

The following steps are applicable in either setting up a new organization or reorganizing an existing organization.

1. Develop an Overall Philosophy of Organization.

Too many managers and supervisors live one day at a time. These individuals lose a long-range perspective because they are so preoccupied with daily activities that they don't have time to think through a philosophy of organization. A philosophy that every design can be improved, every skill increased and every method improved creates an environment of change. These changes make it imperative that effective managers constantly think about organizing in a way that will better serve the economic performance of their company. Your philosophy will influence your unit objectives, which will help determine your organization structure.

2. Think About the Needs/Wants of Your Customers in Developing Your Structure.

Your thinking should begin and end with the needs and wants of those who are willing and able to buy your products or services. Your operation and your company's profitability depends upon customers coming into your business, not your competitor's. Your employees must all be organized with the thought of working toward customer satisfaction. For without customer satisfaction you will have no markets, and without markets you and your employees will have no business to go to. This doesn't mean that marketing dominates your organization, but it does mean that all departments and people must be coordinated to understand how their work activity contributes to customer satisfaction. Therefore, think about organizing your area with the focus on customers.

3. Inventory Work Activities and Group These Activities.

In this step, you list the many activities that are needed to run your unit. Activities such as general administration, order processing, personal selling, sales promotion, recruiting, inventory management, public relations, financing, warehousing, purchasing, pricing, transportation, sales forecasting, records management, production scheduling, inspection, material/equipment control, advertising, product planning, credit management, community relations, marketing research, etc., may be included in your list.

You must then group these activities as to what is best for you given your organization size and resources. For example, keeping employee records could be an activity of your bookkeeper even though your competitor has a personnel individual doing it.

In this step, you are (a) determining what the employees will do and (b) why the employees will do it. The information you gather will enable you to develop job descriptions that will save you unnecessary confusion and conflict in the future.

4. Determine Number of Work Positions with Associated Job Descriptions and Titles.

Based on Step 3, which really is a job analysis, you are now in a position to put your thoughts into a written job description. Many managers and supervisors don't take this step and, consequently, cannot understand why they have explosive people problems. Others believe that they will somehow restrict employees with written job descriptions. However, when you consider that this step sets the stage for supervision, control, disciplinary action, employee orientation and instruction, grievances and personnel policies, the cost is well worth the benefits of this document. This document should contain a list of common duties, authorities (authorization to do something) and accountabilities (what measured results you are to achieve). To prevent any misunderstanding, it is also a good practice to indicate on each job description that the person's position will also have an obligation "to perform other assigned duties." It is another good idea to assign description titles to created positions for internal and external communication purposes. One company that I was associated with used the term "marketing representatives" for its customer-service people when "customer-service representatives" would have been the better title. To further compound confusion, they called their accounting group the customer-service department. This department title created confusion for many employees when they needed financial information. Customers wanted customer service, not marketing, and employees wanted accounting, not customer service.

5. Develop Job Specification Requirements.

Following your job description, which clarifies accountabilities and control, you are now ready to develop job specifications. Briefly, a job specification lists the skills, experience and education required of people and the working conditions affecting them. This step forms the foundation for your wage and salary administration, interviewing process, safety programs and employee training and development workshops.

6. Review Your Planning Process.

Your objectives help determine your strategy, which in turn helps determine your organization structure. At least once a year you should review those changes that have taken or are taking place in your industry. This may require new objectives, which may lead to a modification of your present organization. You may now have to hire a computer jock to solve some accounting or control problems, and clarification of this new position must be communicated to all personnel involved. In going through the planning process, new opportunities may present themselves, which could also cause a change in your present organization. Don't fear change. In fact, the organization that isn't thinking about a more efficient organization design is probably a dying organization.

7. Establish Policies and Procedures.

The inefficient development of well-written policies is often a weak link in many business organizations. Too often companies have no written policies at all, or they have policies for every combination and permutation of events. Another pitfall is that policies are generally written by staff people who also write procedure manuals. It's no surprise that many policies are really procedures in disguise. It's difficult to define the concept of a policy, but I like to think of a policy statement as an action decision operating management makes that serves as a direction code in support of key objectives. Procedures, on the other hand, are the specific steps to be taken in specific situations. Policies should affect behavior, place limits on people but give people freedom to act within those limits. Policies do allow discretion of thought and are designed to save you time. You will not develop your people if they have to come running to you for every decision. So policies should be current, they should be clear and they should be written by those individuals who must implement policy.

To aid you and your people in the development of policy statements that communicate, I've found that the following format is very helpful:

1. State your *policy*   —your decision or action.

2. State your *purpose*   —what you want to accomplish.

3. State your *program*   —a brief outline of systems.

4. State your *procedure* —a series of steps to implement purpose and assignment of responsibility for administering it.

Not all policy statements will be as detailed as the suggested format. However, in utilizing a consistent format you will have the advantage of improving policy, and you will gain a competitive advantage over your competition.

8. Make Sure You Stay Efficient.

Excellence in management, like the skill of a craftsman or artisan, is often a function of knowing when and how to use a particular tool in shaping the organization. Are parts of your organization now relatively unproductive? Are some of your people losing their drive? Are empires or roadblocks developing? What structural problems are developing that inhibit the interaction of key people? Are inequities in layoff or hiring policies and procedures developing? Answer these questions and make the necessary changes.

To help ensure your organization's effectiveness, conduct a periodic organization audit. An organization audit is a diagnostic tool for identification of specific strengths and weaknesses within your organization. Some individuals may not react to this idea with the same enthusiasm as participating in the annual golf tournament, but it is necessary if you are serious about your management. An organization audit is not an accounting audit. Through asking specific questions related to activities, grouping of activities, coordination, assignment of jobs and delegating appropriate authorities, one can get a good idea as to whether the organization design is still effective.

This audit can be conducted by a project team representing many functional areas. However, it is sometimes desirable to obtain an outsider's objective opinion. You should constantly be thinking about designing your organization around well-defined work activities if you want to operate a profitable business.

ACTION EXERCISE

1. Review your company's and departmental goals/objectives.

2. Inventory and analyze work activities.

3. Develop your structure.

4. Assign work to structure units.

5. Staff your organization.

ACTION STEP

8

How to Measure and Improve the Performance of Your People Through Setting Standards and Conducting Performance Reviews

It's illogical that anyone should be appointed to a responsible position without a clear idea of the standard of performance expected.

—COLONEL LYNDALL URWICK

Earl Nightingale, quoted in the *Monthly Letter of the Royal Bank of Canada*, has pointed out that "every moment of every day, we live surrounded by standards. The roofs over our heads and the walls around us are supported by beams and joists of standard width and thickness; we wear clothing of standard sizes from our hats to our shoes. Standards govern the design and performance of the things we use— furniture, utilities, appliances, tools and vehicles. There are even standards to monitor the cleanliness of the air we breathe." From this we can see that standards play an important role in our lives and that the development of these measures or standards is a crucial activity for business success.

Standards will help you direct your limited resources (manpower, materials, money, machinery and time) to those areas where the rewards for your efforts will be the greatest.

Standards make it easier for you to discuss performance with your people when you conduct a performance review. Standards make it possible for your people to rate their own job performance and initiate self-development activity. Standards can improve communication between you and your subordinates through a discussion of expectations. In addition, standards make it possible for you to measure your own performance, spot comers and, at an advanced stage, base and justify salary increases for your people.

Despite all of these benefits, if you were asked the question, what is the highlight of your management career? I'd wager that the farthest thing from your mind would be the setting of standards or the conducting of a performance review. There are many reasons for this, including a general lack of understanding of what standards are or of ways to establish standards. But when it comes down to basics, the main reason that many managers and supervisors don't set standards is the fact that we are not very good at it. In addition, we are out of our comfort zone when we conduct a performance review, because we lack a system to help us. We assume that our subordinates understand what is expected of them and how well their job must be done. It is this assumption that gets us into trouble. And on the other hand, a subordinate assumes that he or she is doing his or her best, but has no guidance from you as to what he or she should be best at. Consequently, subordinates fall into the "busy trap" and produce activities but not many results. Then, observing their performance, we assume that our employees don't seem to want to improve. This cycle gets repeated so that a couple of years down the road you are still doing the same thing over and over again.

Your productivity and the performance of your people is in part a matter of setting standards. Therefore, it is important that you, your boss and your people understand this process. Don't be negative and assume that this is a very time-consuming process because you have to set standards of performance for those three, four or five areas where a high degree of success is needed. These few areas generally represent 65 to 80 percent of the job. Setting standards for the rest of the job will be uneconomical and too time-consuming.

STANDARDS OF PERFORMANCE

Standards of performance are written statements of conditions or results jointly arrived at that should exist when a job or project is satisfactorily completed. These results are usually measured in terms of quantity of output, quality of output, the time needed to produce the product or service and the costs of the needed resources. Other measures can be used, and will vary from type of position or management level to type of work.

Many people will resist the development of standards either because they believe their work, like a priest or minister, cannot be measured or because they don't appreciate the benefits. However, high-performance people are rarely, if ever, satisfied with their performance at work. Those who resist must first be convinced that setting performance standards is nothing but a tool for getting people to think constructively about their work and their jobs. It is a tool to get them to see what degree of performance is expected and where and how their work can be improved.

The only effective way I've found to effectively agree on standards with the doubting Thomases is to get these people talking about their jobs with a skilled and patient meeting chairman. This technique calls first for individual discussion of high-payoff areas (or group discussion if your situation demands it) followed by a group brainstorming session. High-payoff areas are those areas where managers and supervisors should be spending their time, effort, energy and talents. This type of session involves having your subordinates thinking about all the areas and activities that they are involved in at work. The list they come up with should include all types of work that they do during the year. They should record what they actually do on the job, then choose the three, four or five high-payoff areas that result in approximately 80 percent of the accomplishments. Next, use the standards of performance criteria. For example, under what circumstances is your performance in high-payoff areas satisfactory? Then list everything that is suggested by the group. At first, it may seem to you to involve too much use of scarce time. However, the cooperating discussion and agreement that results is well worth the effort. As with all brainstorming sessions, don't criticize the ideas as they are suggested. You want to communicate to your people that all of you, including yourself, can do your work better. Then prune the list that was produced by your own people. The measurements agreed upon are your list of standards. The next time you go through this session your people will know the objective and set standard procedures. Your meeting will be more time-efficient and productive.

A basic format for you to use could take the following form:

Employee Name: _____   Position: _____
Period: _____   To: _____
Prepared by: _____   Date: _____

High-Payoff Areas	Standards of Performance
(What I must do)	(When I've done it satisfactorily)
1.	Quality:
	Quantity:
	Time:
	Cost:
	Planning:
	Communication:
	Other:
2.	Add or substract from above criteria.
3.	Same as above.

CONDUCTING PERFORMANCE REVIEWS

A well-conducted performance review will meet the needs of your people, make you a more effective manager or supervisor and enable you to gain the commitment and trust of your people. From my consulting experience in establishing standards for industry, I know that managers, supervisors and business owners will only accept this tool when they see it helping them accomplish their goals and objectives. They want results. The model presented is a time-tested, reliable success model. It will identify those areas where change is necessary, and where change has the best probability of paying dividends for you. It gets results.

On the other hand, I have observed situations where managers and supervisors found it difficult to sit down with employees and tell them how they are doing. They viewed this motivational, informational and administrative tool as a burden. Employees pick up this feeling via nonverbal and verbal communication and also become dissatisfied with this process tool. What is therefore necessary for many managers and supervisors are some practical guidelines to handle performance reviews that are efficient and effective. This chapter suggests a three-pronged strategy, plus a follow-up to get better results. Simply stated, the strategy is: (1) get your organization ready—the preliminaries; (2) get yourself set—final preparation; and (3) go—your action plan.

GET YOUR ORGANIZATION READY

With the many changes in your company's environment and the increasing complexity of our society, your operation will become more complex. Consequently, the need for well-qualified men and women in business becomes more apparent. To help you meet the need in identifying, measuring and developing people, a performance-review system is the suggested ticket. You and your organization then must address yourselves to the following basic questions:

1. What is the quality of our current job performance and the depth of management talent in our company?
2. What individuals appear to have the potential for taking on more responsibilities?
3. What are these individuals' strengths and limitations?

In getting your organization ready, there are certain dimensions you should consider. These are: (1) What is your purpose/objective in having this tool? (2) What are you going to measure? (3) How will you measure it? Let me suggest that (a) your purpose be to improve the quality of work performance via training programs and performance reviews; (b) that you measure employees' actual work via standards of performance, not personality traits; and (c) that you keep an incident file or develop a simple chart to show you at a glance what's happening.

This approach provides you with a mechanism to help people develop themselves, spot minor problems before they become major problems and be a vehicle for salary adjustments, management succession or other objectives later on down the road.

GET YOURSELF SET

In preparation for the performance review, here are a few proven guidelines for you to consider.

1. Do you have up-to-date job descriptions? The problem with most job descriptions is that they are too *general*. However, it is often assumed that employees understand their *specific* duties and responsibilities. Consequently, jurisdictional disputes arise while other jobs go begging for help. Even if you don't have an up-to-date job description, it will still serve as a communication tool for you.

2. Have standards of performance been established and communicated to your people? This is a major failing on the part of people who call themselves managers. Too often they keep their expectations locked up in their minds and somehow assume their employees will get the message without benefit of discussion.

3. Invest time in preparation. This is an investment that will pay dividends. You prepare for your other important meetings. Meetings with your customers, budget meetings, operations meetings and others. It becomes very apparent if you don't prepare for performance-review meetings. Once you say something, speaking before you think it out, it's difficult to erase that remark. By preparing, you will know how to make your employees feel important and appreciated. Otherwise, without preparation, your people will figure out that if you don't care, why should they.

4. Give advance notice. Several days in advance, ask your employees to review their standards/goals/objectives, establish timetables and new work objectives, and be prepared to discuss job projects, problems and other work concerns. It's very upsetting to your people if you tell them as they are leaving work that you'll huddle with them in the morning on their work performance. If it's a typical situation, something had gone wrong during the past week, and your employees will assume that they are in for criticism and that you will have forgotten all the good things they achieved since the last review.

5. Assess your behavior toward employees. Have you been doing your job in explaining *why* various jobs or activities are important, and explaining the *overall picture* as to how employees' tasks fit into the organization? Did you give authority, agree on deadlines, provide for controls, and so on? Was your behavior a roadblock to the person's performance? Where could you have been more helpful?

6. *Review incident file.*   An incident file is a file you keep on employees that records the exceptionally good or exceptionally poor work-performance activities. We tend to forget all of the good work habits and accomplishments. Consequently, by viewing the file we can be positive in our approach. Our key to a successful review is establishing a nonthreatening atmosphere. Remembering only the negatives destroys this atmosphere.

7. *List strengths and limitations.*   We all have strengths and limitations. As professional managers we must attempt to maximize the strengths of our employees and minimize their limitations or weaknesses. By having a good idea of individual strengths and weaknesses you are in a better position to improve the effectiveness of your people and, therefore, your company.

8. *Develop tentative list of work objectives and development goals for the next period.*   This will help establish clearly in your mind what work you think can be accomplished during the next work period. By having discussions with your employees you can jointly determine whether or not your thoughts are realistic.

GO! (WHAT TO DO DURING THE REVIEW)

I have divided this section into three subsections, each of which has its own guidelines.

A. Your Opening Comments

Assuming you have arranged for your calls to be taken care of, thank each person for coming and create a friendly climate via discussion in sports, family or other interests of employees.

Next, review the purpose and anticipated benefits of the meeting. Say something like, "We're here to fix problems and not place blame," and "I'd like to help you achieve your individual goals, and see what course we can navigate before the next review session." It's also a good idea to ask for feedback to see if employees understand the purpose and benefits of meeting.

B. Your Review of Work Performance

Suggest to employees that he or she: (1) summarize work activities engaged in; (2) appraise own performance in each area; (3) discuss problems and concerns; (4) list opportunities for improvement; (5) tell how you can help; (6) list resources needed.

Then give your input to employees as to whether you find that their work performance:

1. made major or significant contribution to the organization.
2. exceeded standards for the job.
3. meets standards for the job.
4. is below standards for the job.
5. is not meeting majority of standards.

For areas below expectations, be *positive*. Make a positive statement: How can I help you meet your sales quota? Not a negative statement: Why are you not meeting your quotas like the other salesmen? Or another positive statement: I think I may be able to assist you in meeting your production objectives, if we focus on such and such. Not a negative statement: Why are you always behind in your production quotas?

Finally, ask for employee recommendations. Your employees have minds in addition to hands. Often problems can be solved by just asking your employees. After you have heard employees' ideas, evaluate them and, if necessary, offer yours.

C. Your Action Plans, Summary and Closing Comments

Jointly set standards/goals/objectives for the next period. Don't be *vague* by saying, "You have to improve your behavior around here" or "You must work harder." Specifically target a work area that needs improvement and discuss a measure and time frame for work to be performed. Summarize the main points discussed and the action plan for the next time period.

End the meeting with enthusiasm. Thank employees for valuable suggestions and past contributions to the company. Express your confidence in those persons.

FOLLOW-UP

1. Evaluate your own performance after the interview. What did you do right? What did you do wrong? How can you manage yourself better next time?

2. Note on your calendar when you will follow up on the action plans you jointly agreed to.

3. Do the required administrative work. That is, update your incident file and summarize your comments and observations for your boss in the matter expected of you.

FINAL REMARKS

I'm often asked as to how often performance reviews are needed. There's no mathematical answer to that question, and my answer usually is as often as needed. However, depending upon the size of your company, the experience of your people and their classification, different suggestions can be made. For new employees or apprentices reviews should occur at least quarterly. For experienced, exempt personnel a review probably is only needed annually. For nonexempt employees you may want to experiment with semiannual reviews.

It is also a good idea not to mix salary reviews with performance reviews. We all think we are doing a good job. Consequently, if salary adjustments are not in line with employee expectations, you have lost the motivational and developmental aspects of a well-conducted review.

Finally, realize that your role requires you to create a positive, nonthreatening climate during the performance-review interview. You are a coach, not a judge.

ACTION EXERCISE

Develop a checklist for yourself. What will you do:

1. Prior to the interview.

2. During the interview.

3. After the interview.

ACTION STEP
9

How to Control Your Costs

*Count the pennies, and the
dollars will save themselves.*
—OLD ADAGE

Does your company go on a witch hunt once or twice a year looking for unnecessary costs? Chances are that you are familiar with the edict to cut costs by the magic number 10 percent. Chances are also that the attitude of your people will be to play the game, tighten the belt for a period, and then it will be business as usual. Many of us have gone through this school of training, and consequently we either build in some fat for our pet projects or develop the attitude that cost control is not really our job. This is unfortunate. It should be fundamental for good management to pay continuous attention to those significant areas which affect operation costs. The key word is "continuous" and not "sporadic" attention. The job of controlling costs is not an easy one, but it is crucial to the economic success of all organizations.

Controlling costs may not automatically gain you entrance into the promised land of super profits, but without controlling your costs you will not survive as a healthy organization. If you don't develop a cost consciousness or take advantage of opportunities to reduce your costs, you probably will jeopardize the existence of your operation and/or your company.

108

COST CONTROL AND THE MANAGER

Although many managers and supervisors recognize the need for cost control, inexperienced managers are not familiar with the process steps of assuring effective control. In addition, new managers or supervisors usually place emphasis on paper controls versus emphasis on systematic review and corrective action. Still others put a low priority on cost control either because past efforts have failed or due to lack of senior-management commitment. However, high-performance managers have discovered that it takes three components for successful cost-control programs. First, there is a need for a formal plan to accomplish activities by specific dates. Second, a systems approach is necessary to coordinate various efforts with the least expenditure of time, effort and energy. Third, employee involvement and senior-management support is required to accomplish results. These individuals view cost control as a major responsibility in using their available economic resources in the most useful and profitable manner possible. They are knowledgeable in the fundamentals of cost control and have an action plan to follow through with their programs. They realize that only by a continual emphasis on cost improvement can they be effective in this vital area.

WHAT IS COST CONTROL?

Too often managers and supervisors view cost control as a short-run project mandated by pressure from senior management to do something about those rising costs. They tend to equate cost control exclusively to mean cost cutting. Costs have a habit of inevitably rising. They may increase due to not controlling manpower, capital, materials or other costs and inefficiencies. However, cost control does not necessarily mean cost cutting. It means evaluating cost in terms of its impact on your profits. You may cut the wrong costs and actually increase total costs. Good managers do not deliberately cut the wrong costs, but without a systematic review with procedures for cost-excess identification, this will happen. Also, cost control does not necessarily mean cancelling entire programs to save a few dollars. But cost control does mean that you operate these programs in a more efficient and effective manner.

Cost control does include looking for effective cost-reduction areas. It means that the manager or supervisor can make use of the widely known Pareto's Law: 20 percent of your time will yield 80 percent of your results. Consequently, you want to spend your time looking for those high-payoff areas where the level of unnecessary costs can be taken out of your cost structure. Your challenge, then, in cost control is to evaluate cost in terms of its impact on profitability and to continually seize opportunities to reduce costs. Only with this philosophy of a continual cost consciousness on your part and on the part of your employees will you be an effective manager or supervisor who operates economically and efficiently. You must make cost control a professional commitment, and make it a weapon for profit improvement.

A PLAN FOR COST CONTROL

Before you think about specifics in a cost-control program, you should think about *where you are*. You should analyze your operations using basic common sense. For example, if your business is labor intensive, do you have a proper assignment of your people? What are your recruitment and selection procedures? Do you have too many employees given your level of sales? If you are capital intensive, is the allocation of funds based on relative need and desired profitability? What improvements in managerial control over capital spending are necessary? Will the MAPI (Machinery and Allied Products Institute) formula help you obtain answers to the question of whether or not to replace capital equipment? If you need a piece of equipment and don't acquire it, it will cost you in other ways. If your business requires major purchases of materials, are you controlling these costs and working with your suppliers to reduce future costs?

1. Focus Efforts on High-Payoff Areas.

Effective cost control can begin with identifying those accounts where costs are apparently excessive. An understanding of income statements and profit-sensitivity analysis are two tools for managers to be familiar with in this area of cost control. Since the basic information source for most managers and supervisors is the income statement, we will analyze this financial statement and then look into profit-sensitivity analysis.

Managing and controlling costs with an income statement makes it possible for you to avoid many reasons for failure. By comparing expenses in one period to previous periods, or by comparing your expenses to industry averages, you can begin to obtain answers to the following questions:

1. What opportunities exist for improvement in your area?
2. Which units in your operation are marginal or unprofitable?
3. How productive are your employees?
4. Are you meeting your objectives for specified elements of costs?
5. Are you in control of your expenses?

The following table provides a sample cost analysis. In analyzing the operating expenses of your unit or company,

IDENTIFICATION OF HIGH-PAYOFF AREAS

	Year "t" Dollars	% of Sales	Year "t-1" Dollars	% of Sales	Typical Firm T/F	Variance Yr. "t" vs T/F
Net Sales	$900,000	100.0%	$850,000	100.0%	100.0%	—
COGS	560,000	62.2	500,000	59.0	60.0	(2.2)%*
Gross Margin	340,000	37.8	350,000	41.0	40.0	(2.2)%
Operating Expenses						
Salaries	120,000	13.3	110,000	12.9	12.0	(1.3)*
Rent	40,000	4.4	40,000	4.7	6.0	.3
Advertising	50,000	5.6	35,000	4.2	3.5	(2.1)*
Selling	60,000	6.7	65,000	7.6	7.0	.3
Handling	17,000	1.9	14,000	1.6	1.5	(.4)
Delivery	30,000	3.3	27,000	3.2	3.4	.1
Total Operating Expenses	$317,000	35.2	291,000	34.2	33.4	(1.8)
Operating Income	23,000	2.6	59,000	6.9	4.0	(1.4)
Other Income	17,000	1.8			1.8	—
Other Expenses	(10,000)	1.1	(15,000)	1.7	0.8	(.3)
Net Income Before Tax	30,000	3.3	44,000	5.2	4.8	(1.5)

*Large variances signal potential improvement opportunities.
( ) = unfavorable variance.

say you notice that labor costs and advertising appear to be too high. You now ask yourself what opportunities exist for improvement in these areas and follow through with corrective action. Another area to be concerned about is the cost-of-goods-sold section (COGS). In a manufacturing firm, the cost of goods sold represents the cost of producing your product. It includes raw materials, purchases, production-labor costs and plant-overhead expenses. For a typical retailer, it is usually thought of as the cost of acquiring goods sold to the customers of the firm. If you are to be profitable, pay special attention to analyzing cost of goods sold as a percent (%) of total sales for your company and your competitors. An analysis of this section will indicate your purchasing and cost-control effectiveness.

COMPARISON ANALYSIS
CHART YOUR COGS VS. YOUR COMPETITORS

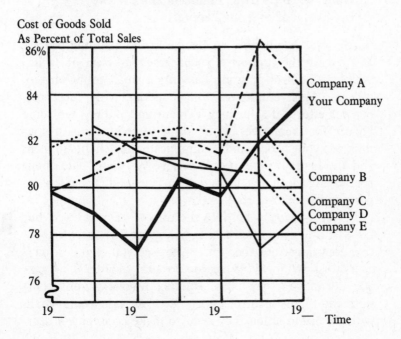

Although comparison with competitors can be inherently dangerous, it often indicates trends. Have a subordinate gather up trade data or, if the companies are large enough, you can obtain this information from published annual reports.

Profit-sensitivity analysis is another tool in a cost-control program. Basically, it asks you to make a 10 percent change in each major element of costs and then calculate the subsequent impact it has on profits. Of course, not every cost element can reasonably be changed by 10 percent. Consequently, there are two steps in this analysis. First, as mentioned, you project a 10 percent change for each factor and, second, estimate how much each factor can actually be changed. This process identifies the factor areas that offer the best opportunity for cost control.

2. Gain the Support of Management and the Involvement of Your People.

Without involving your people in the planning process and having the support of management to clear obstacles, your cost-control program has only a small probability of success. Most employees will cooperate with your cost-control efforts if you involve them and if they see some benefit for themselves. Your job is to give positive recognition to your people and communicate the benefits to them and the firm. If your people believe you don't care about cost-saving ideas, few ideas will surface, and this will hamper you in your efforts.

Be careful not to fall into the trap of "Do as I say, but not as I do." Too often managers expect their people to be cost conscious, but then employees see you or other managers wasting money. What you do speaks louder than what you say in your pep talks. Another way of gaining commitment to cost-control efforts is to provide your people with the information they need to make cost-control decisions. In my work, I often hear from subordinates that their managers or supervisors want them to control their respective costs but don't provide them with feedback information.

3. Select the Right Approach.

Whichever approach you use has its advantages and limitations. No single approach will be best for every situation. Therefore, it's necessary to look at a few approaches and understand what can or cannot be accomplished in your circumstances. The most common approaches include (1) cutting budgets by x percent, (2) the use of a technical staff, (3) annual profit planning, (4) a team approach, and (5) building in a cost consciousness.

The edict approach produces fast results and on the surface is nondiscriminatory. Everyone has to cut costs by x percent. However, this approach can penalize those units that have their costs under control. Consequently, they may have to cut the wrong costs, which will result in profit reduction. Although this approach is considered administratively fair by some managers, it does create dissention. The use of a technical staff provides the talents of many people, usually on a full-time basis. This group can create cost-saving models and focus on opportunity areas. Unfortunately, some technical groups are more interested in state-of-the-art techniques than in addressing your specific problem. In addition, it will forfeit your chance to develop a cost consciousness within your own people. The annual profit-planning approach can build enthusiasm and sharpen your managerial skills. However, it often takes too much time, generates too much paperwork and creates friction among departments. The team approach can be very effective. It can provide talented men and women with different backgrounds to deliver a 360-degree look at cost-control situations. It also provides excellent management training for these individuals. The disadvantages include the difficulty in obtaining a percentage of their time and the chance that the team approach may not be accepted by current organizational relationships. The cost-consciousness approach makes it the responsibility of everyone in the organization to do battle with unnecessary costs. It places a continuous emphasis on cost effects to the benefit of the operation. The limitation is that managers are not often adept in transferring this philosophy as a way of life into their operations.

4. Develop Action Plans.

If you are going to be successful in controlling your costs and thereby improving profitability, you need an ongoing action plan. Your action plan is at the heart of your planning process in establishing a cost consciousness among your people. The action plan represents the decisions you make on *how we are to get there*.

In the planning process, you have established cost-control objectives based on a situational analysis of your operations. Your objectives were set in those areas where control of costs would have the best impact on the profitability of your operations. Your objectives were specific, measurable, realistic, assignable and time-related. The next step in your action plan is to obtain the commitment of your people. It is through commitment that you will see productivity improvements. For new employees, cost-control accountabilities should be written into the job description. For others who are either upgrading their skills or interested in salary increases, make efforts to establish a review of costs in your performance reviews.

If you can tap an employee need, you can motivate that employee to be more conscious about wasteful practices. One of your fundamental functions is to motivate your people toward departmental and organizational objectives. Use your motivational and communication skills in moving your people into cost consciousness.

Finally, in your action plan, hold regularly scheduled meetings and set priorities for cost improvements. Set up cost-control circles. Select a small group of your employees and meet for about an hour to discuss cost problems, investigate their causes and come up with recommended solutions. If you have the authority, proceed to take corrective action.

OTHER COST-CONTROL TOOLS

Sequential analysis and ratio analysis are two other tools that managers and supervisors should be familiar with in controlling their costs. Each tool enables you to identify the basic ingredients making up each major cost component. Your objective is to convert problem identification areas into action projects that result in improved profitability. Your company's profitability, of course, also depends upon innovative marketing programs, but cost control can show dramatic increases in profits. For example, if your net profit before taxes is 3 percent, for every dollar in sales your cost is 97 cents. If you can save just 1 cent, your profit goes from 3 to 4 cents—a 33 percent jump in profits. This is a good result obtained quickly.

Sequential Analysis

Sequential analysis is also known as decision-tree or logic networks. It helps you plan a course of action or helps you isolate courses of the area you are investigating. It can also investigate the dollar values of all subfactors that allow you to identify where you have leverage in cost-control opportunities. For example, let's assume you have identified your distribution costs as being too high relative to the typical firm in your industry. So you set an objective to reduce distribution costs. Then you ask yourself, what are the major components of distribution costs? Then you can take each of those major components and break it down into subcomponents.

SEQUENTIAL ANALYSIS DIAGRAM

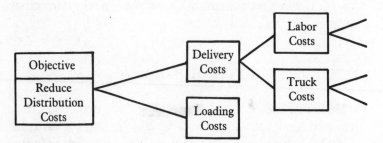

Having identified the costs and the reasons for the costs, you develop your plan to take corrective action.

Tests of Performance

Your income statement is rich in providing you with operating income that will make you and your people more effective. Although income-statement ratios are valuable tools, as with all ratios they should be used with a healthy skepticism. A qualitative feel is also important in interpreting ratios. Ratios are more informational and decisive than specific figures. For example, two of your departments could both have $25,000 in net income. However, if one unit had sales of $100,000 and the other $1,000,000, a different picture of profitability emerges.

Manager Income Statement Ratios

Any system of cost control should include an analysis of profitability. These ratios express management performance in the form of key relationships upon which business or operation success depends.

Profitability Ratios

There are many variations of profit ratios. However, some key ratios include:

A. Gross Profit Margin

$$\text{Gross Margin} = \frac{\text{Net Sales} - \text{COGS}}{\text{Net Sales}}$$

When profit is talked about, it's important to know what profitability level is being discussed. I once had a franchise salesman tell me about all the money I was going to make if I invested in his franchise. When asked if it was bottom line profitability he was talking about, he gave a definite yes. However, after a few more questions, it became obvious that he was talking gross margins. I don't think he was being dishonest, he just didn't know the distinction between gross and net profit margins. The net-margin ratio would be net income to net sales.

B. Return on Total Assets

$$\text{R.O.A.} = \frac{\text{Net Income}}{\text{Total Tangible Assets}}$$

As a manager or supervisor you should be interested in the return of the assets that you have control over. This ratio represents a test of your organization's ability to earn a profit. The ratio is the return on assets ratio. Some "experts" suggest that the net-profit figure used in this ratio should be net profit before deducting interest expense, since it represents a payment to creditors for the use of borrowed funds. Net profit and net income are interchangeable terms.

C. Return on Investment   Those who are serious about using a R.O.I. criteria as a measure of management effectiveness should read C.A. Kline's and Howard Hessler's article "The Du Pont Chart System for Appraising Operating Performance" (NACA Bulletin No. 33, August 1952). This is a concise yet in-depth way of looking at the operating performance of various departments in a manufacturing organization with large capital commitments. Briefly, R.O.I. can be thought of as the earning power of an organization.

$$\text{R.O.I.} = \text{Margin on Sales} \times \text{Asset Turnover}$$
$$= \frac{\text{Net Income}}{\text{Net Sales}} \times \frac{\text{Net Sales}}{\text{Total Tangible Assets}}$$

This equation considers the utilization of assets and the profitability on sales. Together they measure operating efficiency. If you apply this equation to your individual lines of operation, you will do a better job in managing and controlling your organization. By tracing through the factors that affect R.O.I., you will understand the flows and obtain better results.

The challenge facing you in the neglected area of supervisory training is to develop a cost consciousness so that you and your firm remain competitive and profitable. You must do more than talk about cost control. You must realize that it is your responsibility to seize profit opportunities and develop action plans to remain efficient and effective. Cost control is a continuous effort.

KEY MANAGER/SUPERVISOR RATIOS

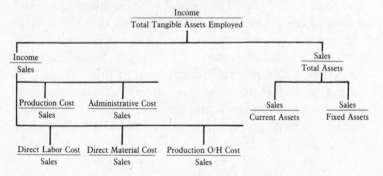

ACTION EXERCISE

Fill in the blanks in the chart below.

Comparative Analysis of Your Operation to the Industry				
Ratios	Your Operation		Industry	
	This Year	Last Year	This Year	Last Year
Gross Profit Margin	____	____	____	____
Net Profit Margin	____	____	____	____
Return on Assets	____	____	____	____
Return on Capital	____	____	____	____
Return on Investments	____	____	____	____
Asset Turnover	____	____	____	____

ACTION STEP

10

How to Increase Your Productivity Through Strengthening Time-Management and Delegation Skills

Time stays long enough for those who use it.
        —LEONARDO DA VINCI

One machine can do the work of many ordinary people, but no machine can do the work of one extraordinary man or woman. Extraordinary individuals know their priorities and achieve results, yet seem to have enough time to develop their people and do the other things that need to be done. These men and women have learned that time is a precious resource and, therefore, shouldn't be wasted. They are not so busy that they haven't any time to plan or think, nor do they fear a loss of control or status when they delegate. They are not interested in making themselves indispensable. Many of these successful individuals report that they owe their success to good time-management practices and to their ability to delegate. Your ability to manage your time and to delegate accountability and authority will be two keys to your success. Thus, good time-management practices and delegation skills are essential in increasing your productivity.

IMPROVING PRODUCTIVITY WITH TIME MANAGEMENT

Simply stated, those who plan the use of their time are more productive than those who don't. Research has shown that most people waste approximately two hours every day. Consequently, efficient use of your time will gain you an extra 30 days a year. Therefore, when you begin to focus on spending your time more effectively, you will become a more productive individual. As a supervisor or manager you give your company your productive time. It's not the hours you put in at work that count; it's what you put *into* the hours at work that counts.

How do you spend your time? Chances are that if you are like most people, you spend your time in those areas where you have the most experience and feel most comfortable. You probably also spend a major part of your time doing those routine or detail-work activities that should be delegated to others. Perhaps you do those things because you feel you don't have the time to explain the details of work to your people or because you simply like doing detail work. Still other managers and supervisors spend their time doing nonmanagement work because it makes them feel productive and needed.

It appears that there is always enough time to do the comfortable things but never enough time to do the priority things. You and I have 168 hours per week or 8,760 hours per year. How we use it is another matter. Time is a unique resource and it is irreplaceable. We should, therefore, constantly remind ourselves *what we should be busy at* or *what is currently the best use of our time*.

Since the days of Benjamin Franklin, time has been associated with money. Franklin said that "time is money." If time is associated with money, it's also associated with profitability. As with profitability, we must learn how to control more of it and how to use it more effectively. If we fail to manage our time, time will manage us. Consequently, we need a systematic approach to organizing this resource.

THE IMPORTANCE OF KNOWING WHERE YOUR TIME GOES

In order to manage time, you must first know where it goes. Many "experts" in time management suggest that you have your secretary log your time for a week period. Although determining how your time is spent is a good approach, this method may not be practical. Either you don't have a full-time secretary, or it's not possible to give someone another add-on job, or, frankly, you don't want someone watching you every moment for a period of time. These "experts" neglect to take into consideration the Hawthorne Effect, namely, people will try harder when they are part of an experiment and, therefore, an accurate reading will not be obtained. Then, too, around budget time or sales-presentation time, you will spend time in entirely different ways.

Consequently, to make an objective appraisal of how you spend your time, you must do it yourself. Someone else cannot do it for you. You want to know what you really do with your time, not what you assume you do with it. There is often little resemblance between what you actually do and what you think you do. However, the fact that you are reading this chapter is a positive step in a program to be more productive. You are now on your way to getting more done in less time.

HOW TO GET STARTED

Your normal day is filled with interruptions. You have to spend part of your time on nonproductive time wasters.

Your boss wants you to chat with a sales person, or an important customer calls you to discuss a nonproblem, or the receptionist sends you calls that you shouldn't receive. Five minutes for this, ten minutes for something else and another five or ten minutes to check on something.

I've learned that I can't control all my time and that I must accept some of these interruptions as part of my day. I realized very quickly that too much organization of time is not workable. However, to get more done in less time, I've discovered that if I think in terms of 15-minute intervals via a time-inventory sheet, I will get more accomplished. I may have to spend an hour with someone to be productive, but in my mind's eye I was very aware of the use of my time and my subordinates' time.

In creating a system that works for you, you may want to start by using a system that, through trial and error, I've found to work for me. The things-to-do-today sheet summarizes and puts into action much of what I know about time management.

You may want to make some adjustments on the Things To Do Today inventory sheet. Then have a month's supply run off.

As the day proceeds, log in your work activities: the time it takes you to get to work, the time you spend reading new product information or information about your industry, time spent with the boss, planning time, developing your subordinates, coffee breaks, maintenance-work activity, writing reports, etc. In addition, you may want to record your energy level during the day.

Keep your time log for at least three to four weeks, and record your activities once every half hour or as circumstances permit. You will be the judge of what works best for you. Do not be in a hurry to start making changes in your daily routine. Your job is to obtain a realistic recording of your time. Only then can you start thinking about managing your time, which means making small changes in how and when you work.

THINGS TO DO TODAY

Date _____

Planning Calendar	Priority	Action	Completed

Specific Things To Do

People To Meet

Morning

7:30	_____
8:00	_____
8:30	_____
9:00	_____
9:15	_____
9:30	_____
9:45	_____
10:00	_____
10:15	_____
10:30	_____
10:45	_____
11:00	_____
11:15	_____
11:30	_____
11:45	_____

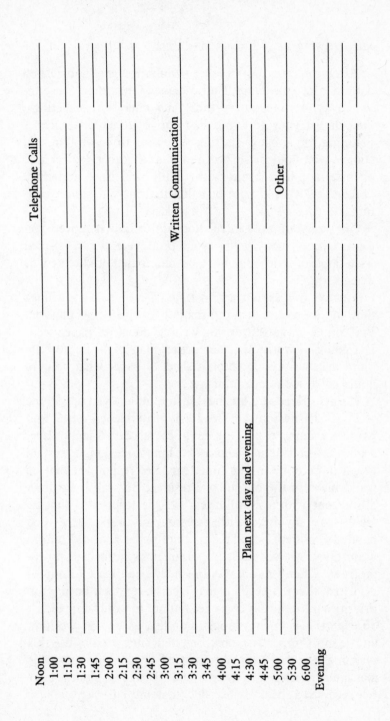

Telephone Calls

Written Communication

Other

Plan next day and evening

Noon
1:00
1:15
1:30
1:45
2:00
2:15
2:30
2:45
3:00
3:15
3:30
3:45
4:00
4:15
4:30
4:45
5:00
5:30
6:00
Evening

After three or four weeks, summarize your job-related activities into meaningful subcategories that make sense for you, e.g., administrative time, customer time, meetings, etc. Or list your activities in terms of functions, such as planning, organizing, staffing, directing or controlling. Of course, you could also broaden your summary to include estimates of time spent with family or leisure activities. Percentages should then be calculated in your summarization.

Analyze your time in relationship to how it moved you toward your goals. Review your time log and ask yourself what job activities can now be eliminated, redirected or delegated to others.

Finally, prepare an action time plan. List those things that you are going to do to make better use of your time. I've found no substitute for writing down on paper what I'm going to work on. Your action plan could be nothing more than writing down on a sheet of paper what you are going to do today or tomorrow.

Herman Krooss, a business historian, enjoyed telling the story of Charlie Schwab, president of Bethlehem Steel, and his paper action plan. One day, Schwab called in Ivy Lee, a business consultant, and asked him to develop a system to get more done in less time. Mr. Lee responded that he could increase the output of President Schwab by at least 50 percent within 20 minutes. Charlie responded that he would pay any fee—within reason, of course. Lee then handed President Schwab a piece of paper and told him to write down the six most important jobs he had to do tomorrow. When Charlie was finished, Lee then told him to prioritize them. Lee then told Charlie to work on his top priorities until the day was over but not to worry if he didn't do everything on the things-to-do-list, as he was working on the most important jobs. Lee then suggested to use this system every day and, if convinced of its value, have his management team also use it. Well, about two months later Lee received a check for $25,000 (in noninflationary dollars) from Charlie Schwab with a note explaining the $25,000 was one of his best investments. The return on investment (R.O.I.) was very impressive.

SOME ADDITIONAL KEYS TO EFFECTIVE USE OF YOUR TIME

As with consultant Ivy Lee's advice, the following are tips on how you can better use your time. Not all the suggestions will be right for you in your circumstances. However, you should find many ideas to help you become more productive.

1. Know Thy Time.   The fact that you are conscious of how you are using your time (administrative, customers, community relations, planning, etc.) will result in giving you more time. This is a necessary condition, and the time log will help you in discovering how you use your time.

2. Avoid Overcommitment.   As mentioned, your normal day will have many interruptions. Therefore, don't fill you calendar too full. When work or social requests start pouring in, learn to say no. Don't allow your subordinates to put the monkey on your back. Bounce problems back to your people, and have them use their creativity in solving their own problems.

3. Control the Controllable.   Do you have to call a committee meeting, or is some other alternative more time efficient? Do you start meetings on time? When people want to say hello, do you greet them in your office or in the hall? Before you go to a meeting, do you know the basic purpose of that meeting? There are more things around you that you control than you realize.

4. Separate Essential from Nonessential.   Separate what you have to do from what you would like to do. Determine your most important activities, and then prioritize them into A-B-C or 1-2-3 categories. Don't get caught in the "comfortable trap" and only take care of the pleasant things.

5. Plan the Day Before.   You may have noticed on the time log, or things-to-do sheet, that there's an entry at 4:30 P.M.: "Plan next day and evening." I've found that toward the end of a day it's best for me to plan the next day's priorities. That way, when I arrive at my desk the next day, I know exactly what I'm going to do and consequently don't get caught in the "busy trap" of memos, phone calls, etc.

6. Find Your Prime Time.   Each of us has a biological clock that pumps more energy into us at certain times of the day. Plan on using this mechanism for tackling those projects that will take a large amount of concentration and effort.

7. Have a Quiet Time.   Set aside a period of each day for thinking and reflecting. As a manager, not only do you have to have your finger on the pulse of day-to-day activities, but you must also be aware of your organization's changing environment.

By forcing myself to have a quiet time, I actually work smarter and save myself time. Some managers have told me that if they take a quiet time they are no good for the rest of the day. If this is true for you, disregard this suggestion.

8. Set Deadlines.   Parkinson's Law states that work expands to fill the time available. This is an astute observation. Set time goals, be ruthless with your time, like a newspaper editor, and you will get much more done.

9. Learn to Delegate.   Delegate those things that you like to do or in which you have experience. When your subordinates give you feedback on those activities, you will know if things are going right or not. By delegating, you will be accomplishing more by doing less.

10. Carry a Three-by-Five-Inch Index Card. One of the most effective time savers for me is to carry a three-by-five-inch index card with my daily priorities on it. Even if one of my main priorities is to have lunch, this card is a constant reminder of those two or three priorities that must be accomplished before the work day ends. Try it and see if you don't agree.

11. Phone Instead of Visit. Whether the person you want is next door or halfway around the world, phone instead of visit. The airlines may not like this suggestion, but using the phone can be an important time-saving tool.

12. See Salespeople Once a Week. Early in my career, salespeople and those who wanted to sell me advertising used to control my time. If they were in the area, they wanted to see me. Usually the meeting took longer than I expected, even when I realized that the product or service was not for the company. Now 95 percent of the time my secretary's response is that I can see them for 15 minutes Thursday morning. Besides saving my time, I've discovered an interesting bonus. When salespeople know that their time is limited, I usually receive a better price for that product or service.

13. Handle Paper Once. Make a decision on every piece of paper you pick up. If you don't, you may pick up the same piece of paper twice, three or more times. Delegate it, ditch it in basket number 13, or do it.

14. Carry a Small Notebook. Many good ideas have been lost and time wasted trying to remember what you've forgotten. By carrying a notebook with you, jot down the ideas as you hear them or think about them.

15. Use a Month/Year-at-a-Glance Calendar.   A favorite time saver of mine is the year-at-a-glance calendar. If this won't work in your circumstances, a smaller month-at-a-glance calendar may be your ticket. It has saved me much time in looking up future events. It will also be a big time saver for you.

16. Have a Purpose and Agenda for Every Meeting.   One of the really big time wasters is not having an agenda for meetings. When side issues come up, as they usually do, without an agenda it's difficult to deal with these tangential items. An agenda will help you stay on target and will save your time and the time of the other people at the meeting. Stick to your agenda, purpose and time schedule.

IMPROVING PRODUCTIVITY THROUGH DELEGATION

How often in the past have you heard that "delegating is a key to successful and productive management"? Are you following that advice? Chances are that in the past your success has been determined by your personal ability to get things done. This is why you were promoted into the role of a manager or supervisor. However, now you must begin to broaden the scope of your management thinking. You must visualize yourself as a leader, not as a doer. It's a big jump from being successful by doing to suddenly switch gears and realize that your success will now be judged by your ability to get things done through the coordinated actions of other people. It's important to recognize this. Your success and productivity will be gauged by getting results *through* people, not *for* people.

HOW MUCH IS YOUR TIME WORTH?

Time is your most precious resource. Use it wisely. You cannot replace wasted time. When it goes, it's gone.

Time Value	
If You Earn $/yr.	Your Time Is Worth $/hr.
$ 10,000	$ 5.00
15,000	7.50
20,000	10.00
25,000	12.50
30,000	15.00
35,000	17.50
40,000	20.00
45,000	22.50
50,000	25.00
55,000	27.50
60,000	30.00
65,000	32.50
70,000	35.00
75,000	37.50
80,000	40.00
85,000	42.50
90,000	45.00
95,000	47.50
100,000	50.00

WHY DELEGATE?

The ability to delegate will be one of your most rewarding experiences as a manager or supervisor. However, initially you will probably have a tendency to believe that the only way to get a job done right is to do it yourself. Your comfort zone is doing, and your promotion was based on your doing performance. Resist this natural urge. It will stifle the development of your people and result in your doing more work. While it might be true that some individuals may not be able to do the job as well as you, this shouldn't be the criterion. The criterion should be that the individual can perform satisfactorily, not optimally. This thinking in delegating work will build morale and give you more time to do the things you should be doing.

When you delegate you are also building an effective team. Delegating by specific *results* enables your people to take initiatives and experience personal and job growth. If you fail to delegate or if, in your delegating, you tell people specifically what to do, your employees will sense this lack of confidence in them. Ultimately, this will lead to poor communication, low morale and lack of timely results.

WHAT TO AND WHAT NOT TO DELEGATE

Productive managers and supervisors understand that they cannot personally look after every detail in their operation. If you are to be effective, you must delegate the details, not to get rid of unpleasant work, but to get results. You also want to delegate those technical, clerical or mechanical tasks to others who are probably more qualified. Your job is to be a manager or a supervisor, not a martyr who feels that he or she has to do everyone else's work. You should delegate those jobs that are indicated in the accountability section of a modern job description. Tasks, projects or activities that will contribute to the personal growth of your people is another area in which to employ delegation. As with good time-management practices, you should delegate those jobs on your time log that can be satisfactorily handled, if not better handled, by your subordinates.

Of course, not everything can be delegated. There are areas where you probably should not delegate. The making of policy, or any specific job in an area where no one else is qualified cannot be delegated. The resolution of conflict, if it cannot be solved by the parties themselves, will be your responsibility. If your boss personally expects you to do some task, it would be risky on your part to delegate it to someone else. Dealing with matters that may result in an unfair labor practice is another area where delegation should not be attempted. To be a productive manager is to be a developer of people. While you may delegate others to train some subordinates due to a specific need for certain skills, your role as a developer of people cannot be delegated. Finally, in deciding what to or what not to delegate, always consider the interaction of people and the situation involved.

HOW TO DELEGATE

Delegation is an art *and* a science. It is a true test of your people skills. Delegation is the science of assigning work with the authority that gets results, and the art of working through people. Ultimately, you are responsible for all tasks and activities delegated. Delegation must include the heart as well as the mind.

Over the years I've found Doran's Six Steps to be very effective in delegating and receiving assigned tasks. The system is as follows:

1. Create the Proper Climate.   This step asks you to explain two "whys": why the job or task is important to the organization, and why the specific individual was chosen. Speak to the individual in terms of benefits, or focus on the unique strengths of why that person was chosen for the task.

2. Paint the Macro-Picture.   Communicate how the job or task fits into the total organization. By hearing an explanation of the big picture, the employee can make those decisions that would usually take up your time.

3. Delegate in Terms of Results.   Your subordinates may ask you *how* to do the job, or you may be inclined to tell the subordinates how. Resist the temptation. Explain to the qualified subordinate that he or she is free to do the job in his or her own creative way. Employees must decide how to reach the specific objectives that you want. Delegate by the results wanted, not the methods to be used.

4. Give Proper Authority.   If a crane is needed, don't authorize a shovel. You are guaranteed failure if you fail to delegate enough authority to do a job. Sometimes this may take a formal letter or, other times, just a phone call. In giving authority make sure that both you and your subordinates clearly understand the degree of delegation granted. In the example given, delegation isn't authorization to go out and purchase a crane for the company. Authority must be specific.

5. Provide for Controls, Feedback and Deadlines.   Providing for controls basically means establishing a feedback system for yourself and your subordinates. Both you and your people must understand what "how are things going" really means. You want to be alerted in time to take action if difficulties arise. On the other hand, your subordinates need information on their performance, and they need your confidence in their ability to perform the work effectively. By setting agreed-upon deadlines, you and your subordinates understand the expectation of what should be accomplished when. You don't want surprises.

6. *Establish a Review Process.*   You and your subordinates made a commitment to achieve results. What was planned to be done and what actually was done can now become a basis for evaluation and discussion. You can evaluate how effective you are in the use of this tool and discuss the productivity, problems and concerns of your subordinates. By means of the review process, you gain valuable information about yourself and the abilities and attitudes of your people. You are now in a position to better organize your total job and get more done with less energy and effort.

A final note: If you let people carry out their own ideas under your direction, they will feel personally responsible and motivated for their success. Their success is your success. Yes, delegating is a key to successful and productive management. Are you making use of this valuable tool?

ACTION EXERCISE

Make a list of the jobs you do. Review the list and choose a job that you enjoy doing. Delegate this job to a qualified individual, and practice Doran's Six Steps.

1. Create the proper climate.

2. Paint the macro-picture.

3. Delegate in terms of results.

4. Give proper authority.

5. Provide for controls, feedback and deadlines.

6. Establish a review process.

About the Author

GEORGE T. DORAN, PH.D is an expert in strategic planning, marketing, and employee and organization development. He has been associated with the American Can Company, the New York Stock Exchange, the Bunker Hill Mining Company, Washington Water Power Company and other companies in various industries. He has taught quantitative analysis, finance, marketing and management courses at the graduate schools of New York University, Duquesne University, Eastern Washington University and Gonzaga University.

He has a BA in mathematics, an MA in economics and finance, and a doctorate in advanced management, marketing and behavioral science.

Doran is author of several articles on management, and is a consultant and guest speaker to many business groups and private corporations. He resides in Coeur d'Alene, Idaho.